COGNITIVE BEHAVIORAL THERAPY

12 STRATEGIES TO HELP YOU OVERCOME ANXIETY, WORRY, PANIC ATTACKS, OBSESSIONS, AND START LIVING YOUR BEST LIFE NOW.

By Roberta Rivera

Table of Contents

Introduction

If you are struggling with negative thoughts, depression, fear, or anxiety, you can take an active role in getting better. Retraining your brain with Cognitive Behavioral Therapy isn't just fluff; there is substantial evidence to support that it works. If you are skeptical, you may be surprised that this book alters your ideas about "positive thinking." You will be able to regain control of your life.

Cognitive Behavioral Therapy (CBT) works from a scientific base. This book will not overwhelm you with lots of empirical data, but it will display pieces of evidence that demonstrate that CBT works scientifically, and it is far more than just a theory of positive thinking.

In the United States alone, more than 40 million people suffer daily from one or more forms of anxiety disorder. Major depressions, phobias, social anxiety—these are just a few examples, but there is a wide variety and many afflictions fall under this category.

One such affliction is Post-Traumatic Stress Disorder (PTSD). Soldiers returning home from war find themselves unable to adjust to the relative calmness of a largely civilian environment. While our most common association with PTSD is soldiers, it is a myth that soldiers are the only people group affected by it. Post-Traumatic Stress Disorder is suffered by a wide spectrum of people worldwide. Businessmen and women, teachers, taxi drivers...no one is immune.

Effects of PTSD can include panic attacks where one is severely frightened to leave home due to external stimuli ramping up the heartbeat and inducing fear where logically one realizes it should not be present. Worse, the panic attacks might just be one symptom of many. Another familiar anxiety disorder is Obsessive-Compulsive Disorder (OCD), popularized by television's detective character "Adrian Monk," whose obsessive attention to detail allows him to see what is wrong with a crime scene (but also forces him to other less desirable habits, like being unable to walk on cracks in the sidewalk or not drinking water for days because he cannot find his particular brand).

These are just a few examples of anxiety disorders, but the real shame is that many people would rather suffer alone than address these issues.

The refusal to seek out help may possibly be because of television's representation of current psychology and psychiatry. In order to better understand CBT, we should clear the air between the two approaches. It is fairly simple.

A psychologist helps you to talk out your concerns, with the assumption that understanding a problem can give you the necessary awareness to combat it. They cannot write prescriptions.

A psychiatrist, however, takes the approach that a large portion of such afflictions are based on brain chemicals and their imbalance, and they can write prescriptions as needed.

Thus, our fear. We may be considered weak for seeking the advice of someone else to help us cope, or we may be numbed and dulled by medication.

While some consider the former school of thought, psychology, to be the superior method, each has its merit and flaws, but we need to understand that Hollywood has done a number on us in the self-help department.

Television depicts padded rooms or Victorian-era face boxes intended to keep the mad folks from biting off another person's face. Sadly, these depictions do more or less reflect the early history of psychology, but keep in mind that during early wars, amputations were performed with a saw and a healthy dose of whiskey.

Sciences evolve, and fortunately for those suffering from an anxiety disorder, this is the information age.

You can get the help that you need, and if you don't want to involve anyone else in your treatment, there is a way that you can get yourself back on track. The days of suffering in silence can be gone if you are willing to give some tried, true, and tested techniques a chance. The techniques have come bundled together under the name that you've heard but perhaps not really explored.

Let's amend this. Let's discuss Cognitive Behavioral Therapy and what it can do for you.

Chapter 1 What Cognitive Behavioral Therapy Consists Of And Its Characteristics

Cognitive behavioral therapy came about as a combination of the behavior therapy techniques developed by Donald Meichenbaum and the cognitive therapy techniques developed by Albert Ellis. It is a therapeutic approach used to treat a wide variety of emotional dysfunctions or unbeneficial behaviors. The major characteristic that distinguishes cognitive behavioral therapy from other therapeutic approaches is that it is much more systematic and goal oriented.

So, while psychoanalysis is more open ended and used to probe into a person's mind; cognitive behavioral therapy uses specific, practical techniques to change the unwanted thought process or behavior. One advantage of being so systematic is that you do not necessarily need a therapist to successfully use the techniques of cognitive behavioral therapy.

A therapist can, of course, be helpful as a guide or source of motivation when things get tough but, in general, you can successfully treat yourself with the techniques described by cognitive behavioral therapy. In fact, even if you do have a therapist, a large part of the work will be done by you since you have to apply the strategies to your everyday life. This contrasts with psychoanalysis, for example, where the therapist does the bulk of the work because it is their job to do the interpretation and analysis.

The reason that cognitive behavioral therapy is so effective in the treatment of so many disorders is because it is so problem oriented. This approach operates on the understanding that negative or harmful thought processes are the primary factor contributing to negative or harmful behaviors and emotions. Therefore, cognitive behavioral therapy targets those thoughts processes. There are two general strategies used to deal with these negative or harmful thought processes.

The first strategy is changing the thought process itself. This involves various techniques (depending on the specific problem at issue) for identifying, isolating, and eliminating a negative thought. Usually, in this process, you also work to cultivate positive thoughts that are meant to take the place of the original negative ones.

The second strategy involves changing your relationship to the negative thought process (rather than changing the thought process itself). This requires you to constantly challenge these negative patterns of thinking or beliefs and thinking consciously about them. That means understanding what sort of errors in thinking (or cognitive distortions, as they are called in cognitive behavioral therapy) are involved. For example, perhaps you are running a slight fever and your first thought is that you have some form of untreatable cancer.

By understanding exactly how a negative thought is flawed (beyond the simple fact that it is negative), you can take the power from it and no longer allow it to control your behavior or your emotional state. This will also help you to tell the difference between rational negative thoughts (such as genuine signs of serious illness) and the irrational ones.

Both of these general strategies are highly effective ways of treating serious problems. In this book, you will learn self treatment methods that combine both so that you can not only strip a negative thought of its power but replace it with more positive ones.

Within these two general strategies, there are a variety of specific methods used which includes exposure therapy, cognitive processing therapy, acceptance and commitment therapy (ACT), dialectical behavioral therapy, and relaxation training. All of these have their own specific methodology but each has the same ultimate goal of greater self-awareness.

We can break the cognitive behavioral therapy process down into six generalized phases:

Mental health assessment: this is an important preliminary step in which you simply work to identify exactly what your problem is. Are you depressed? Are you anxious? Are you suffering from a phobia or addiction? Assessing your current mental and emotional state will already bring you one step closer to achieving full self awareness.

Reconceptualization: this phase is more based on the "cognitive" side of cognitive behavioral therapy. It is in this phase that you begin identifying and challenging the negative thought processes which are causing the problem (or problems) you identified in the first phase.

The specific techniques for doing this depend on your specific problem.

Skills acquisition: in this phase, you begin the process of learning the new coping skills you will use to both overcome the current problem and get through troubling situations in the future without falling back into the same negative behaviors you are used to. These coping skills can be either cognitive or behavioral skills and will depend largely upon the specific problem you are dealing with.

Skills consolidation and application training: in this phase, you put together a plan using the specific coping skills you have learned and want to use in your cognitive behavioral therapy treatment. Then, you start practicing the skills according to the plan you have created. This is typically the most intensive and time consuming phase because you are essentially retraining your brain and trying to develop new habits.

Generalization and maintenance: by this phase, you will be more or less used to the new coping skills you have been working on throughout phases 3 and 4. Now, all you need to do is make them a part of your daily routine and use them in all challenges that you face rather than just those relating to the specific problem you were treating.

Post treatment assessment and follow up: if you have been working with a therapist, this is something that you will do with them. Otherwise, you can essentially do another mental health assessment to see what progress you have made and what areas you may still be struggling with. This may seem like an unnecessary step but it is actually very important. By doing a post treatment assessment, you can take the time to appreciate how far you have come. You can also see what problems you might still be struggling with and go through these 6 phases again to treat those.

All in all, the duration of these six phases and the whole cognitive behavioral therapy process in general will depend on the severity of the problem. However, in most cases you will begin to see positive signs of change in your thought process and behavior in as little as 6 weeks. And after about 6 months, you will notice much more dramatic results. Typically, if you work at it consistently, by the end of the 6 months, the positive skills you have been working on will have become more or less habits (meaning you will be around phase 5 or 6 of the process).

Because the ultimate goal of cognitive behavioral therapy is to achieve greater self awareness, you will actually continue to use these techniques long after your problem has been treated. This is because cognitive behavioral therapy is not so much a one-time treatment as it is a method for changing the way you think about and deal with the challenges and obstacles in your life.

It provides you with positive coping skills (and a technique for making those coping skills into habits) so that you are not only treating the problem currently at hand, but also giving yourself the strength and skills you need to prevent any problems from happening in the future.

Chapter 2 History of CBT

The father of experimental psychology is Wilhelm Wundt and thanks to him, we have the first lab for psychological research at the University of Leipzig. Also, the psychotherapy, as its know today saw its appearance in Vienna as a result of Sigmund Freud's work. Actually, when Freud Arrived in America in the year 1911, the psychoanalysis completely disrupted the whole psychiatry field and the point was reached when more than 90% of psychiatrists in America started to practice how to perform psychoanalysis properly. However, skepticism towards psychoanalysis and its ability to provide a solution has already been in motion since the 1950s and during these times, alternative psychotherapeutic methods started appearing and among these was CBT.

CBT was developed with contributions from people that used to use psychoanalysis as therapy and these people weren't happy with psychoanalysis and therefore they wanted to contribute to the development of something better and that is how CBT spread so quickly through Europe and became one of the prevalent therapies for solving problems of patients throughout the world.

The proper model of CBT appeared in the 1970s and even though it took some time for CBT to appear, it started to evolve really quickly and much quicker than the models such as behaviorism that was pioneered by John B. Watson in 1920s. One reason for this is the fact that CBT isn't strictly limited to the domain of psychology and it was a lot more flexible and it consisted of other fields of science as well, which made it possible for new variants of analyses to emerge.

The first appearance of CBT was by itself a large shift from the therapy models that were established and mainstream at the times, but there were still a lot of advancements afterward which ensured that no aspects of cognition were forgotten about. The second generation of CBT is where CBT got its current name as cognitive behavioral therapy since that time presented a combination of cognitive and behavioral techniques.

There were three generations of CBT throughout history. The first generation of CBT can be seen as taking a stance against traditional therapies at the time which were based on the principles of psychoanalysis and humanism. The first attempts of CBT were already focused on the actions and behaviors that weren't useful and techniques that were based on science were used in order to combat those behaviors. An example of this would be someone who is afraid of public speaking which actually means that that person is afraid of being criticized and judged. What was attempted to be accomplished by CBT at the time was to actually gradually expose individuals to uncomfortable contexts so that anxiety and discomfort would be eventually reduced and mitigated.

As the 1970s were nearing the end, it became more and more clear that CBT was a real deal and that it was here to stay and more and more journals and researches started to cover CBT which led to CBT being introduced into behavioral approaches. It also helped that CBT had, at a time, a lot of supporters in the Association for the Advancement of Behavior Therapy.

At that time, it was also proposed that what should be the focus of research was how humans learn and what actually has an influence on learning since this is what would have a real impact on the second generation of CBT. The basis of this research was the belief that how humans are conditioned is affected by an individual's cognitive and verbal capabilities instead of it all being automatic. It was considered that learning was influenced by elements such as attention, awareness, expectations and linguistic skills. It was considered that people needed more sophisticated models about conditioning instead of those that could be used for animals which was the case for the earlier 20th century. One of the issues was the fact that some things, such as peoples capabilities for words and language, weren't taken into consideration even though those abilities are pretty unique. Therefore, it was necessary to focus more on the cognitive side of things.

As a result, the 1960s saw the emergence of cognitivism which certainly shook up the field of experimental psychology and changed how things were done and viewed. The cognitive capabilities were now at the forefront of the psychological research and they weren't simply seen as a byproduct anymore. That is how the second generation of CBT came to existence in 1977 and the principles that emerged were a lot more flexible and internal attributes such as thinking and emotions were taken into consideration when trying to figure out how people act. It was, therefore, concluded that people can think and adapt their actions for different contexts.

By the beginning of the 1990s, there already existed a lot of knowledge and understanding about how thinking can be distorted for some people and what can be done and which techniques could be used in order to rewire automatic thought patterns. If someone is anxious about something, the exposure should be gradually introduced and increased so that anxiety for certain circumstances would be reduced. Automatic thought patterns should also be questioned.

In conclusion, the fusion between two generations of CBT was what enabled the idea of CBT as we know it today to appear and to be accepted as a form of therapy that is focused on expectations, perspectives, systems of beliefs, cognition and not just behavior on the outside.

Chapter 3 How to Change Your Core Beliefs with CBT

Our core beliefs are at the center of the person that we are, i.e., our beliefs about ourselves, others, and life as a whole. Our core beliefs determine how happy we feel about ourselves, our capacity to get along with others, and our potential to achieve the dreams that we hold for our future.

Considering the power that our core beliefs wield, it is critical for every person to have core beliefs that serve to improve their lives, instead of destroying them. Sadly, many people struggle with negative core beliefs, and they ultimately lower the quality of their lives. For instance, if an individual has a core belief along the lines of "I'm foolish", they will shun opportunities that would have led them to great heights and be trapped in a life of mediocrity.

Our core beliefs are the absolute truths and fundamental convictions we have formed about ourselves throughout our lives. To change how you feel, think, and act, you first have to alter your core beliefs. The origins of our core beliefs are varied, but for the most part, they originate from our early childhood. If our dads used to beat on us and call us foolish, we might have internalized the belief that we are stupid. Getting rid of our core beliefs is an extreme challenge, but if we are self-motivated and patient, we can achieve it.

The following are the guidelines for altering our core beliefs:

Deal with One Core Belief at a Time

You can't possibly get rid of all your core beliefs at once. The trick is to deal with one core belief at a time. You want to start with the most powerful core belief. This is the belief that pervades nearly all of your life. Once you identify it, you have to work out a schedule for eliminating this core belief. For instance, if the most dominant core belief of yours is, "I'm a loser", prove yourself that you're no loser. Make a schedule that will guide you in handling various aspects of your life. You want to be in total control.

How Does It Affect Your Life?

Understanding how a certain core belief affects your life will motivate you to change your circumstances. Banking on your introspection, find out how your core belief negatively affects both your personal life and general life. For instance, if you believe that you're ugly, you might not be the most confident person around. Moreover, it can cause you to isolate yourself from other people. In that sense, you lack social support because your core belief holds you back from fitting in with the rest. Understanding the effect that your negative core belief has upon your life is a catalyst for ridding yourself of that negative core belief.

How Much Do You Believe Your Core Belief?

Some of the core beliefs that we hold are utterly ridiculous. Although the conscious mind would view them with suspicion, when it comes to the unconscious mind, it's another story altogether. The unconscious mind gives much weight to our core beliefs. You are supposed to reflect hard and find out how much you believe your core belief to be true. In this exercise, be as honest with yourself as you possibly can, and don't let your ego ruin what you are working on. On a scale of one to ten, rate the extent to which you believe a core belief to be true. Recall various events or experiences that support your level of conviction.

What Is Holding You Back from Changing the Core Belief?

There are three main reasons why we fear changing our core beliefs: fear of failure, fear of uncertainty, and fear of change. If we have kept a certain core belief throughout most of our lives, what will happen if we get rid of it? And more importantly, how will we cope if we fail? To get rid of a negative core belief, you have to be emotionally invested. Becoming conscious of what is holding you back from changing your core beliefs is a great step forward.

Find Ways to Disprove Your Core Belief

Now that you have identified your core belief, and established to what extent you believe in it, the next challenge is to look for evidence that contradicts your core belief. By disproving your core belief, you send a message to your subconscious that this core belief is inaccurate. The subconscious will take notice of the evidence and start altering this core belief. For instance, if one of your core beliefs is, "I cannot make money", go ahead and learn a skill and monetize that skill. When you get money, you're free to point out to your subconscious, "See, I can make money." Eventually, your subconscious will drop that core belief.

Find a New Core Belief

When you are certain that your core belief is fallacious, it's time to get rid of it and create a core belief that captures the truth. For instance, instead of saying, "I hate people," you might say, "I enjoy my own company." That way, negativity is eliminated. Instead of saying, 'I'm a loser," you should say, "I'm quirky."

Explore How Your Life Will Change Thanks to Your New Core Belief

Now that you have acquired a new core belief, explore how it will help you change your life. If you have stopped viewing yourself in a negative light, you might want to think that you are poised to rise to the heights of success – something you never thought possible.

Chapter 4 Adapting Your Behavior and Applying the Principles of Cognitive Behavioral Therapy

We have covered a little about the cognitive changes that you will need to make but very little on the behavioral side. In this, we will go through how you can change your behavior in order to further improve the benefits of cognitive behavioral therapy. We are going to cover a technique known as Behavioral Activation.

This technique is based around the idea that increasing your participation in activities that you find pleasurable will improve your mood. This is particularly effective for conditions related to stress, depression and social anxiety, where isolating yourself can actually reinforce the problematic beliefs and make it harder to reintegrate yourself.

Basically, you end up in a never-ending cycle – you don't feel like going out because you are stressed and/ or depressed and so you don't go out. The lack of social interaction and lack of engagement in pleasurable activities increases the feelings of stress and/ or depression.

Behavior activation is used extensively to treat phobias, anxiety and depression. It is also helpful in improving your self-confidence and helping you find meaning in your life. It can also entail physical activity and this in itself is beneficial to your mood.

This does not always mean actually engaging in actions that involve physical exertion – it rather means that you step out of your routine and do something different. It is either based on doing something that you find pleasant and enjoyable, like meeting with your friends, or doing something that will give you a sense of accomplishment, like cleaning your home.

Even when an activity is not something that we enjoy, like cleaning, if it gives us a sense of accomplishment it can also be useful in improving mood. The type of activity undertaken will depend on the condition being treated.

Someone who is suffering with depression, for example, is likely to lack the energy or willpower to engage in more activities. Getting them to undertake smaller tasks that are enjoyable will be more likely to achieve the results that are desired than insisting that they undertake a task that they won't really enjoy.

On the other hand, someone suffering with low self-confidence may have the energy to undertake tasks but may be anxious about their abilities to complete the tasks successfully. It may therefore be more useful to identify tasks that allow them to achieve a sense of accomplishment, even if they find these slightly unpleasant.

Finding Your Activity

What you start with is going to depend on what you are trying to change. The first step is to look at what activities you are going to include. To start off with, look for activities that you will actually enjoy doing.

What hobbies have you enjoyed in the past? Is there anything that you liked doing but stopped, for whatever reason? Is there anything new that you would like to try? Are there activities that you enjoy but would like to do more of?

Alternatively, you can look at things that you want to accomplish, like getting your taxes in on time. Again, these may not be things that you have fun doing but they are things that are important to you. Think about how satisfying it is to be able to cross things off your To-Do list.

Is there something that you need to do in order to improve your current quality of life? Learning a new job skill, cleaning out your junk room, etc. are all things that might qualify here.

Whatever task or activity you choose, make sure that it is something that is important to you. Let's say, for example, your parents are always saying that you need to get out more. If you feel that this is important to you as well, then take their advice. If, on the other hand, you are doing this just to make them happy, you are unlikely to follow through consistently.

Choose things that are especially important to you – not something that other people think should be important to you.

Here are some ideas to consider:

Visiting your friends and family and scheduling fun activities with them.

Finding a club in your area that caters to something that you are interested in, such as photography.

Attending religious services.

Going to an exercise class of your choice.

Spending time with animals or getting a pet of your own.

Eating out.

Stimulating your brain by doing puzzles, playing games, etc.

Taking up a physical activity of your choice like hiking or swimming.

Doing charity or volunteer work.

Taking up a hobby that you enjoy – such as knitting, painting, etc.

Going for lessons in something that interests you, like cooking, art, etc.

Starting some DIY projects to improve your home/ living space.

Finding a task that needs to get done like getting your license renewed, etc.

Top marks go to activities that you both enjoy and that give you a sense of accomplishment.

Setting Activity Goals

Now you need to set goals for yourself when it comes to your chosen activity. Let's say that you choose to take up photography again. How many times are you going to go out to practice photography? How will you fit it into your schedule? How long will you spend on each session?

When setting these goals, it is important to be realistic. Start out small to begin with and ease yourself into the process. Let's take the photography hobby again – setting yourself a goal of doing an hour of photography a day would be unrealistic when you are starting out. Setting a goal of going out for an hour a week would be more manageable.

You want it to be as easy as possible to incorporate the new activity. If you have to drive two towns over to attend a meeting, for example, it may be difficult to follow through when your motivation is low. Set a realistic goal, set a date to start and plan around that.

It is essential to do some planning when it comes to your chosen activity. Think about what possible obstacles might get in the way and come up with a contingency plan. What will happen if you cannot do the activity on the day you planned to originally?

Having a back-up plan is important. Let's look at photography again – what happens if it is raining on the day you plan to go out? Is there some way that you can salvage the situation? If you don't feel like doing the planned activity on the actual day, any small obstacles can be used as excuses – planning around the obstacles gets rid of the excuses.

It is also helpful to come up with facilitators. Facilitators are things that encourage you to get something done. You could, for example, arrange to go to a photography meeting with a friend. Or maybe you could sign up with a rewards program that gives you points every time you go to the gym.

Choose something that will encourage you to follow through with your plan.

Volunteering can be especially rewarding in this regard because you get to achieve a sense of accomplishment and meaning in your life. Perhaps you are not motivated enough to take on a hobby for yourself. If that is the case, the idea of being able to help someone else might be enough of a motivating factor to get you started.

Graded Exposure

When it comes to a situation that you are anxious about, graded exposure can be particularly helpful. Basically you start off with an activity that causes you little stress and work your way up as your confidence improves.

Let us say that you suffer from social anxiety, for example. The idea of joining a club might terrify you so you start with something a lot easier, like striking up a short conversation with a cashier at your local store.

Once you are confident with that, perhaps you could look at one on one interactions that are a little more involved, like speaking to your hairdresser, etc.

The idea is to approach the situation gradually so that you improve in small stages. Think about a child learning to ride their bike – they start off with training wheels, in the driveway, they work their way up to balancing on their own and then riding for longer distances.

It is very important to choose a first step here that is pretty easy and that doesn't seem very challenging. The more scared you are by the idea, the less likely you are to actually follow through with it.

It is also vital to be patient with yourself and give yourself plenty of time to master each stage. This is more like a marathon than a sprint – you don't have to rush to the next step before you are ready.

That said, you do need to plan progressions and follow through. When you have reached a relative level of comfort with the current stage, you do need to try the next step up. While you don't need to rush, you should also not stagnate when it comes to making progress either.

Reducing Activities That Are Not Beneficial

In much the same way that you want to increase the activities that help to improve your mood, you also want to decrease the activities that dampen it.

These might not always be as easy to identify because they might not seem to directly affect your mood. Let's say, for example, that you sleep too much. This might not seem to have much of an impact on your mood but it is actually a kind of coping mechanism, a way of avoiding certain situations.

In some cases, these might involve behaviors that are actually overtly harmful, like getting drunk every night or taking too many pills. In other cases, these might be less overtly harmful like avoiding applying for a better job because you are anxious about the interview.

If a behavior or activity has a negative impact on your future – whether this is through causing physical harm or through lost opportunity, it needs to be addressed.

Here again, doing a cost-benefit analysis is extremely helpful. It may be uncomfortable or even unpleasant to address this in the short-term but it is worthwhile if the long-term effects warrant it.

Chapter 5 Recognizing Negative Thoughts And Cognitive Distortions

The first step of putting CBT into practice is recognizing negative thoughts. This can be surprisingly difficult. They are often referred to as "automatic thoughts" because they spring up without much regard for why or how. In order to change them, you must find out where they come from.

Automatic negative thoughts can be sorted into separate categories, known as cognitive distortions. Knowing these can help you identify the negativity and find the root of it. They're known as distortions because they aren't actually based in reality. They are thoughts that your brain automatically produces, perhaps based on past experiences or biased beliefs. Unlike in psychoanalysis, in CBT the cause of the cognitive distortions isn't important. The event that caused them has already occurred and cannot be changed. However, the distortions can be challenged and dismissed, until your mind learns not to create them.

Cognitive distortions are almost always negative and exaggerated, yet convincing. Even though they seem true, once you dig into them, you'll realize that they are not based in reality. They serve no good purpose and only fuel pessimism. It's worth stopping to take a look at any negative thoughts that cross your mind, and seeing if they fit any of the categories listed below. There are also some that may not fit neatly into one of the categories – the true test is whether the thought is based on realistic thinking, and if it serves any positive purpose.

Most people suffer from at least a couple of cognitive distortions. However, they are strongly tied to mental disorders such as depression. In those with depression, the cognitive distortions are more prevalent and have a greater effect on mental health. Those that aren't as strongly affected are usually able to dismiss the automatic thoughts quickly or don't put much value to them.

Take a look at the list of cognitive distortions and examples, and think about which ones may apply to you. Some may jump out at you immediately, or be ones that you already know you experience. Some may surprise you, however, and you'll learn something about your automatic thoughts.

All-or-Nothing Thinking

This can also be known as polarized thinking or black-and-white thinking. There are no in-betweens in this type of thinking. Everything falls to one side or the other of an extreme scale. Things are seen as black or white, never gray. This leads to increased negativity towards anything on the "bad" side of the scale, and ignoring the middle ground that is likely more reasonable.

Examples

•	Either loving or hating people you meet

•	Considering yourself either perfect or a complete failure

•	A situation is either the best or the worst

Overgeneralization

This is the belief that one or two instances of something means it is a pattern, disregarding the complexities of life. It is the same type of thinking that can lead to stereotypes of large groups of people. However, this one is on a smaller scale. It leads to negative thinking about the perceived pattern.

Examples

•	A friend misses a dinner date with you, so you think they'll never make it to any commitments

•	You receive a low grade on one test, so you think you're stupid and won't pass the class

•	Your boss talks to you on two occasions about small mistakes, so you think you're a failure and will never do your job right, or that you'll be fired

Mental Filter

Someone experiencing this distortion will discount anything positive to focus on the negative. When critiques are offered to them, they only take away the negative comments and disregard the positive ones completely. This leads to low self-esteem, doubt, and believing others only see their negative aspects.

Examples

•	In a performance evaluation at work, you completely focus on one negative comment, despite the multitudes of positive ones

•	You only take away the negative comments and what you need to change from a critique on a paper you wrote

- You focus on one negative situation with your significant other, and despite the years of positive situations, believe your relationship is over

Discounting the Positive

This is similar to the mental filter, but instead of not acknowledging the positives, they are seen as false. This distortion can be particularly damaging, because in spite of all evidence to the contrary, only the negatives are seen. Even having the positives pointed out to the person will not convince them otherwise.

Examples

- You receive a positive yearly review at work, but believe it is only because your boss is trying to be diplomatic, and you don't actually deserve it

- When a friend compliments you, you assume they're just saying it to be nice, and not because it's true

- When receiving criticism on a project, you believe the "false" positive points are only there to soften the true negative ones

Mind Reading

Mind reading is a form of jumping to conclusions. It is when someone assumes they know what others are thinking or feeling. We can often pick up body language and other cues to guess what others feel, but this goes beyond that to the point of playing "psychic." The sufferer believes people are thinking negative things about them, with no solid evidence. Those experiencing this distortion believe that others are always thinking the worst of them, leading to doubt and low self-esteem.

Examples

•   Your boss frowns slightly when you hand him a report, so you think he dislikes what he has just seen and is upset with you

•   A pair of people standing near you start laughing, so you assume they're making fun of you

•   A stranger on the subway scowls at you, so you think you've done something to offend them

Fortune Telling

This is another example of jumping to conclusions. In this case, the person is predicting the future with no evidence, usually in a negative manner. It is again playing "psychic" and focusing on one negative outcome, rather than the possibility of a range of outcomes. Constantly believing in a negative outcome means there is no joy in doing things, and can contribute to depression.

Examples

- Your friend takes you to see a movie you've never heard of, and you go in assuming it won't be good

- You believe that your flight will be cancelled at the last minute and you won't be able to take your vacation

- You see clouds and assume it will start raining soon, ruining the outdoor party you were about to go to

Catastrophizing or Minimizing

These are two sides of the same coin, always leaning towards the negative. Catastrophizing is inflating the importance of a small negative event, and believing it to be a sign of worse to come or a failure. Minimizing is reducing the importance of a positive event to support a negative belief. Catastrophizing often feeds into fortune telling.

Examples

- You receive a raise at work, but it isn't very large, so you believe you're doing poorly at your job (minimizing)

•	You break a glass you just bought, and think how clumsy you are and how badly you've messed up, and that the store will surely be sold out by the time you can get a replacement (catastrophizing)

•	Normally good at basketball, you make a small mistake in a game, and believe you've lost your skill and will play poorly from now on (catastrophizing)

Emotional Reasoning

This is believing that one's feelings are reality. Typically, we can recognize that how we feel doesn't necessarily mean it's true. However, those experiencing this distortion accept them as facts. This may be one of the most common distortions, manifesting in people with normally healthy ways of thinking without them realizing. It can lead to assuming the worst of people and situations, and increasing negativity.

Examples

•	You are angry at a friend, which to you means they definitely were in the wrong

•	You feel scared or anxious in the middle of the night, so something bad is about to happen

- You feel lost and hopeless, so you won't be able to resolve your problems

Shoulds

Most thoughts that include the words "should," "ought," or "must" fall under this category. This is a sneaky distortion that not everyone recognizes as unhealthy. We can apply this to ourselves, with thoughts about what we "should" be doing as opposed to what we are doing. Typically, this brings on feelings of guilt and inadequacy for not meeting those expectations. This can also be applied to others, by thinking of what people "should" be doing. This leads to disappointment and anger, as we have no control over the actions of others.

Examples

- You feel you must lose weight before you will be considered attractive

- A friend called to cancel plans at the last minute, and you think he should have called you earlier

- You feel your boss ought to thank you for all the hard work you've done on a project

Labeling

This is a greater version of overgeneralization. It's when someone applies a label to another person or situation based on a small characteristic or event. We can also apply these labels to ourselves. It is a way to judge value based on little information. Labels applied to ourselves can lower self-esteem, and applied to others can breed resentment or misjudgment.

Examples

•   You label your boss a "grumpy old man" after he has a bad day

•   You call yourself a failure after missing one assignment

•   You decide that you're stupid after not scoring well on a test

Personalization

Personalization is assuming that you are the center of thoughts and situations, regardless of evidence to the contrary. Many things are taken personally, and the person takes the blame for any bad scenarios. This causes guilt and unhappiness, and a reluctance to engage in similar situations.

Examples

- Your friend disliked the movie you took them to see, so you feel that you should've taken them to another one and it's your fault

- Your boss is in a bad mood, so you think it must be because of something you did

- At work you receive a company-wide email with a reminder about proper parking, and you believe that it was because of one day that you parked in the incorrect spot

Control Fallacy

This can manifest as thoughts of having no control over one's life, or having complete control and therefore blame for everything in one's life. Either way is equally bad, as they disregard that no one has complete control or absolutely no control in any situation they're in. In the first instance, outside sources, other people, or something as mysterious as "fate" are seen as having the ultimate power. In the second, the person holds themselves accountable for every little thing that happens and the happiness of those around them.

Examples

•	Your poor work performance is your boss's fault, rather than yours

•	Your friend is going through a hard time, and you feel responsible for fixing it

•	You believe that fate controls your life path, so there is no point in putting in any effort

Fallacy of Fairness

This is the false belief that the world operates on fairness. The person believes that everyone will always be treated with equality, and is resentful and hurt when that isn't the case. While most of us would like everything to be fair, in reality, life is too complicated for that.

Examples

•	Your friend never repaid you the $5 you leant her, so you justify taking $5 out of her purse without her knowledge

•	You didn't receive any recognition for how hard you worked on a bake sale, making you bitter and unhappy at the event

- You worked overtime a couple of nights, and think it's fair that you take off the same amount of time the next week, and become angry when your boss says that isn't how it works

Fallacy of Change

This is when a person expects others to change for their benefit. It typically comes with the belief that your happiness relies on others, so they must change their ways in order for you to be happy. This often leads to selfish thoughts, and to disappointment and resentment when others won't change. More so than some of the other distortions, this one can push people away from the sufferer. Others will view them as selfish and perhaps even controlling.

Examples

- You believe that if your significant other cleaned more often, you would be happier and therefore a better partner

- You want your friend to cancel plans they've already made to go out with you

- You think your coworker should stop wearing his favorite cologne because you dislike the smell when you walk past his cubicle a couple of times a day

Always Being Right

This distortion may also be referred to as perfectionism. The person believes that they must be right, regardless of anyone else's thoughts and feelings, and being wrong is the worst failure. Debates or arguments are escalated from being a question of who's right to a battle of wills. The person may believe that their opinion is fact, or disregard evidence that says they are wrong. This is often at the expense of others, or makes others regard the person as combative and unfriendly. Always being right brings on unnecessary anger and conflict, and makes it difficult to maintain healthy relationships.

Examples

•	Internet commenters that argue well past the point of reason

•	Arguing with your spouse about chores and refusing to back down or admit defeat

•	Starting arguments when someone else states an opinion you disagree with

Magical Thinking

This is the idea that once you reach a certain goal or point, something positive will happen for you. Setting goals for yourself is important to improving, but this distortion says that as soon as the goal is reached, you'll get the outcome you desire. Common ways the thoughts appear are "Everything will be better when I _____," or "If I _____, I will _____." This leads to frustration and negativity when the goal can't be reached soon or is too lofty, and disappointment and resentment if the desired outcome doesn't appear.

Examples

•	When I lose thirty pounds, I'll find the man of my dreams

•	Once I get a new job, I'll be happier and everything will come together

•	Everything will be better once I'm rich

Heaven's Reward Fallacy

Heaven's reward fallacy can go along with the fallacy of fairness. It can also sometimes be referred to as "karma." Essentially, it is the belief that any self-sacrifice, suffering, or hard work will be rewarded justly. Part of this can be belief that one will be rewarded in the afterlife, but it also applies to expecting rewards in the near future. The person with this belief will set aside their own happiness and desires in the hopes of an appropriate award. As well as contributing to immediate unhappiness, this can also lead to frustration, resentment, and negative feelings when the desired reward isn't received.

Examples

•   If you work more overtime than anyone else, you'll be rewarded with a larger raise

•   Signing up for a volunteer opportunity with the expectation of being rewarded, rather than for the cause

•   If you set aside your own problems to help a friend with theirs, they will soon repay you

Double Standard

A double standard is when you believe you should have a higher standard than others. This usually involves comparison to others, and though you approve of their actions or thoughts, you feel that you must do better than that. It can be a form of "one upping," but more often it is a way to set a bar for yourself. This bar is usually difficult to reach, and you hold no one to it except yourself. This brings on the pain of not reaching lofty goals, and the disappointment and negativity that comes along with it.

Examples

•	You congratulate your friend on receiving a B on the test, but believe your own B is a failure as it could have been an A

•	You don't mind when others aren't dressed up at the grocery store, but you feel that you need to wear nice clothes and makeup to go out in public

•	You're happy for your colleague that met their project deadline, but beat yourself up for not finishing early

Do any of these cognitive distortions sound familiar? It's likely that at least a couple resonate with you. It will take some work to identify some of them. The problem with cognitive distortions is that they pop up of their own accord and can be quite convincing. However, they'll likely fall apart under close scrutiny since they aren't based in reality. The only purpose they serve is to increase negative thoughts and berate yourself.

Begin a thought log in your journal. Keep it with you, and write your thoughts as soon as they occur whenever you're able. If you can't keep it with you, be sure to write as soon as you can to keep the situation fresh in your mind. If you find yourself forgetting to use the log, pick a set time each day to fill it out, and set an alarm to remind you if necessary. You can create columns to organize the separate, or use whatever method you prefer. Write down the automatic thought that you had, as well as the date and time. Then, write down the situation that led up to the thoughts. Be as factual as you can for this, leaving the emotion out of it. Describe it as though you were an outside observer with no stake. For the next, write down the emotions that you felt. Also consider any physical symptoms you may have felt. For example, anger can come with an increased heart rate, or depression can bring fatigue. Next, describe the behavior that these thoughts and feelings led to. Be subjective when writing about your behavior or actions, and fully honest. Finally, identify which cognitive distortion(s) apply to your automatic thought. Be detailed and truthful in what you write. Your journal is a judgement free place that no one else will see, and it is a crucial tool in your therapy. Right now, we're not aiming to change any of these things; we're simply acknowledging that they exist, and therefore training our brain to detect them more easily.

You might find that some of your cognitive distortions end just by noticing they exist. Sometimes we have thoughts that we don't realize are wrong or harmful, but as soon as we know they are and why, we can get rid of them. That won't always be the case, though. For the distortions that are sticking around, you'll need to learn to challenge them.

Do you like this book? it would be important for me if I could leave a short review on amazon. thank you!

Chapter 6 Benefits of Cognitive Behavioral Therapy in Addiction Treatment

A mind that has been ruined by drug addiction is the perfect breeding ground for negative thoughts and other emotional health issues. Managing challenging thoughts and emotions is hard enough for a sober person, but when you consider a drug addict, the experience is ten times worse. Thankfully, drug addicts can benefit from CBT. Cognitive behavioral therapy has been shown to achieve long-lasting results in the treatment of various addiction types.

The following are some of the benefits of CBT in addiction treatment:

Provides a network of support

Cognitive behavioral therapy allows addicts to have a network of support which is very crucial during the recovery phase. The average addict, if not given positive encouragement, could easily relapse into drug abuse. Therapists are there to offer positive encouragement and gently guide these people toward full healing. When addicts realize that no one cares about them, they are likely to go back to seek solace from drugs. Having a network of support is critical for not only avoiding a relapse but also ensuring general emotional well-being. People are social beings. Thanks to the support network, addicts have someone to talk to.

Increased Positive Thought Patterns

Addicts often struggle with a negative thought pattern that makes them feel helpless; ultimately making them go back to doing drugs. An addict struggles with many bleak thoughts and feelings. However, through the power of positivity, they can overcome their mental and emotional health issues. CBT puts an emphasis on positivity. The more positive an individual is, the less likely they are to slide back into drug addiction. Therapists help addicts overcome their conditions by planting positive thoughts in their subconscious. This helps addicts become positive by default. And whenever they experience emotional troubles, they have someone to guide them.

Enhancement of Self-Esteem

Low self-esteem is one of the reasons why people turn to drug and alcohol. They want to forget their misery and their helplessness. But cognitive behavioral therapy helps addicts develop a great self-image. As their level of self-esteem goes up, they find less desire in escaping reality through drugs and alcohol. They are happy to be themselves. Therapists constantly reinforce addicts' self-esteem and thus raise their desire of wanting a better life than the one they presently have. To get rid of an addiction, the affected person must have the desire of wanting to change their personal circumstances, and this desire becomes natural when an addict's self-esteem is given a boost.

Learning to Resist Peer Pressure

Since we are social beings seeking peer acceptance, it is extremely challenging to resist peer pressure. It is challenging for the average person, and ten times more challenging for the drug addict. Cognitive behavioral therapy equips addicts with the skills for overcoming peer pressure and focusing on their important life goals. When it comes to resisting peer pressure, they are trained first to imagine saying NO to their peers, and then actually saying NO within a controlled environment. By the end of the training, they won't have any difficulty saying NO to both their peers and anyone else who might be a negative influence.

Cost-Effectiveness

Cognitive behavioral therapy is one of the most affordable addiction treatment methods. Some other treatment methods like rehabs have in-house arrangements for the patient. These treatment methods can be incredibly expensive. Cognitive behavioral therapy can be conducted on an outpatient basis and achieve great results. This treatment method is even covered by insurance plans. Cognitive behavioral therapy is not one-sided. For its success, both the therapist and the patient must work side by side. If the patient is not cooperative, then the treatment will tumble down. Cognitive behavioral therapy is not complicated. It involves general procedures that lead to the restoration of health. There are no expensive or complicated tools required.

Gradual Steps

Overcoming an addiction is no walk in the park. It is a time-consuming quest. Remedies that claim to offer instant results are obviously misleading. In cognitive behavioral therapy, a therapist introduces new principles to the patient as they advance through the treatment. There are principles set aside for the beginners and principles set aside for those who have reached the advanced stage. Walking through these steps, the patient's resolve is strengthened, and they are less likely to run back to drugs or alcohol than patients who have been through any other treatment model. The beauty of cognitive behavioral therapy is that it doesn't advertise itself as a quick fix. It takes real effort to achieve results. However, the effects are long-lasting.

Continuity of Normal Activities

Cognitive behavioral therapy is done on an outpatient arrangement. The patient is free to indulge in other activities for the rest of their time. This is unlike rehabs where patients are held in a campus, effectively suspending their daily engagements such as going to work. With cognitive behavioral therapy, a patient is neither separated from their family nor do they have to seek leave. Because of its flexibility, more people are willing to take this treatment method. And if the sessions are scheduled at night, then your day will run without even a slight hitch.

Gradual End to Therapy

Cognitive behavioral therapy places the entire focus on the patient. The concepts and exercises may be adjusted in accordance with how the patient is faring. In some forms of addiction therapy, the treatment lasts only for a specific amount of time, and then it is cut off. This kind of arrangement doesn't take care of patients who would take ordinarily long to recover fully. In cognitive behavioral therapy, the first few weeks are typically intensive, but as the patient's condition improves, the therapist finds less need to have intensive sessions and focuses on going at the patient's speed of recovery.

Chapter 7 CBT as A Treatment for PTSD

If you have lived through or witnessed a shocking, scary or dangerous event, you might develop a condition known as Post-traumatic Stress Disorder. These traumatic events range from losing a house to fire, losing a loved one, or surviving a road accident. The more an event excites horror, helplessness, serious injury or death, the more potent the PTSD.

Main Symptoms of PTSD

Re-experiencing symptoms: this is where a person relives the terrible experiences in their minds. If the traumatic event they went through had been a loss of their house by a fire that even claimed one of their loved ones, the affected person might start having flashbacks of the event. Traumatic events tend to make a person feel helpless, and when they come back to haunt them in the form of flashbacks or intrusive thoughts, the affected person feels drained of energy. They lose their capacity to move on with the rest of the day after re-experiencing the traumatic event through their mind's eye.

Avoidance symptoms: sufferers of PTSD tend to avoid events or situations that might lead them to think back to their traumatic event. For instance, if someone had lost their loved one through a water accident, whereby their boat capsized, the sufferer may actively avoid ever getting into a boat again. This is because if they entered the boat, they would have no peace at all, a mixture of fearing that whatever happened to their loved one might happen to them, and getting to relive the horrific event in their mind.

Hyperarousal symptom: if you have lived through a traumatic event, it can modify your nervous system in such a way that you become too sensitive. For instance, you could become anxious at the ring of a loud noise, or the flash of a bright light. These are merely your survival instincts kicking into gear. Additionally, you could have trouble falling asleep or getting to concentrate. Such problems would embitter your life, eliminate happiness, and potentially ruin your life too.

Cognition and mood symptoms: another obvious sign of PTSD is an inability to remember the exact details of the traumatic event. The rush of adrenaline you had experienced back then might be responsible for blocking out some of the details. Then you might experience guilt or blame someone for what happened. If you think that you had a chance of mitigating the trauma, but failed to, you will experience an immense amount of guilt. Additionally, PTSD can make you lose interest in activities that you once enjoyed.

There are a number of ways of treating Post-traumatic Stress Disorder, but one of the most effective ways involves the use of CBT. Actually, it is believed to be the most effective form of treatment, with people living with PTSD getting rid of their symptoms in as short as twelve sessions.

The following are some of the methods used in treating PTSD:

Prolonged Exposure

If someone has lived through a traumatic event, it is only natural to want to stay away from the thought patterns that would call back those traumatic memories. However, this treatment method seeks to do just that: expose the person to the memories of the trauma for an extended amount of time. The logic behind this treatment method is that once the person with PTSD confronts their fears, they will eventually stop being bothered. However, if they keep running away, then the traumatic memories will hold a lot of power over the individual. As a subject of numerous scientific studies, this treatment method has received praise for being effective in eliminating re-experiencing symptoms, anxiety arousal, and avoidance of PTSD-arousing stimuli. Positive results can be achieved by the third session.

Cognitive Processing Therapy

When a traumatic event takes place, the affected person might develop various maladaptive assumptions that will increase the potency of their trauma. Cognitive processing therapy is used in detecting and restructuring the maladaptive patterns in their thoughts. This method helps people with PTSD find meaning out of the trauma, and it also helps decrease their anxiety and boost their self-esteem. Cognitive processing therapy has been shown to have a high success rate of curing PTSD symptoms. To a large extent, the success of this treatment model is down to the sufferer, i.e., they must be cooperative.

Seeking Safety

When you live through a traumatic event, your emotional makeup might become twisted. For instance, if you survive a road accident, you will become an extremely sensitive person. Something as ordinary as experiencing a bump while riding a car will suddenly make you fearful, cause a flood of emotions, and it will take a long time to return to normal. Seeking safety helps people to overcome their emotional dysregulation and cope with their extreme fears. One of the ways of curing emotional dysregulation is through practicing mindfulness. When your mind is focused on savoring the present moment, it is less likely to jump back to the traumatic past.

Eye Movement Desensitization Reprocessing

EMDR is much like prolonged exposure, except that it utilizes eye movement exercises. This treatment was popular a few years back but seems to have fallen out of favor with therapists since the evidence came out that the eye movement exercises achieved nothing. However, some therapists still employ this method of treatment. In keeping with the tradition of prolonged exposure, the sufferer is made to relive their trauma, through their minds, and then the therapist guides them in performing various eye exercises.

Chapter 8 Common Issues CBT Deals with Most Effectively

Anxiety

While feeling anxious or nervous from time to time, during moments where you are unexpectedly called out to perform in front of your peer group, or when dealing with an unexpected financial worry, are perfectly fine. Some people feel this way constantly, and even minor issues can send the feelings of anxiety climbing ever higher. If you feel as though the anxiety you are experiencing goes above and beyond what can be considered normal, then you might be living with some type of undiagnosed anxiety disorder. Despite the serious toll that this can take on those who deal with it on a regular basis, it can be difficult to determine for yourself. This is largely because anxiety can take many different forms, and the line between normal and excessive can be difficult to determine precisely.

The most common example of an anxiety disorder is excessive worry over common occurrences. The trouble then becomes deciding on a level of worry that is "normal" and a level that is "excessive". When it comes to generalized anxiety disorder, the most common type of anxiety disorder, excessive does have a precise meaning. If you would say you have had anxious thoughts more than 50 percent of the time for the past six months, then you may be dealing with an undiagnosed anxiety disorder.

This anxiety needs to be severe enough that you would classify it as interfering with your daily life to the point that it is causing physical issues such as fatigue or stomach pain. If you don't feel as though your physical symptoms are all that severe, then you may still be dealing with generalized anxiety. It can also make itself known by causing extreme dysfunction in your everyday life.

Another crucial indicator that you may have an anxiety disorder is if you find yourself having a hard time sleeping at night. It may be that you are agitated or otherwise unable to stop thinking about certain things that need your attention, regardless if they are all that serious in the grand scheme of things. In fact, approximately 60 percent of all of the people who experience generalized anxiety experience these symptoms. Alternately, you might find that you fall asleep easily, but when you wake up, your mind is immediately filled with anxious thoughts that you have a hard time quieting.

One symptom of generalized anxiety that is easy to miss, especially if you have been living with it for a prolonged period of time, is excessive muscle tension. This can also be difficult to pin down as it will likely manifest for everyone in different ways. This could be anything from clenching your jaw, to hunching your shoulders to balling your fists. A related symptom that many people with generalized anxiety experience is a general dislike of being touched.

Panic attacks are another symptom that can be confusing for many people, simply because it is not one that everyone is going to experience. Instead, if you happen to experience panic attacks on a regular basis, and your triggers don't seem to be related to specific fears or sensations, then there is a fair chance that an anxiety disorder may be to blame.

Depression

While everyone feels a little depressed now and then, there is a serious difference between feeling down in the dumps from time to time and feeling a level of complete and utter despair that is so severe that it seems as though it is never going to end. Depression can make it virtually impossible to enjoy the good things in life, or even remember that the good things in life exist at all. When you are in the clenches of a depressive episode, even making it through to the end of the day can be a Herculean feat. The good news is that things can get better and recognizing the symptoms and connecting them to yourself is a great first step.

Officially, depression is a common and debilitating mood disorder that is far more than simple sadness. Rather, depression changes the way that your mind processes common events and activities, altering the way it functions and you feel, in the process. If left untreated, it can interfere with your ability to work, eat, sleep and generally enjoy any facet of life. The feelings of hopelessness that it brings along can be so intense that it can seem impossible to believe that any relief is in sight.

If you do feel as though you are battling depression, the first thing you will want to do is to pay closer attention to your moods and emotions. If you are truly suffering from depression, then your brain will have a hard time regulating your emotions properly, which means you may find yourself dealing with extreme levels of guilt, hopelessness, despair, numbness and more. You may also feel as though you are worthless in general, though if you look for the source of these feelings, you will likely come up empty handed as well. You will also likely be more irritable than normal, which can result in a shortened temper and an increase in verbal or physical altercations.

Besides dealing with lots of unwanted emotions, you will also likely feel the need to withdraw from social activities that you previously enjoyed, along with your support group as well. Those who are battling undiagnosed depression often feel an urge to retreat from the world at large, in hopes that isolation will make what they are dealing with more manageable. This is rarely going to be a good choice, however. Without a means to connect to the outside world, the problems that they are dealing with tend to seem worse, not better, and then things are only magnified when they have no other viewpoint to listen to but their own.

If you still aren't sure if you are depressed, the next thing you are going to want to keep in mind is that you will likely be experiencing behavioral changes as well as mental ones. This does not mean that you are going to see these changes materialize all at once, however, and will instead slowly appear and grow more pronounced over time where you may not even notice them as a result. As such, you will likely find it helpful to track your behaviors over time to ensure any negative habits you are aware of don't get any worse, and no new ones appear at the same time.

Common signs of depression that you are going to want to be on the lookout for include erratic behavior such as either a dramatic increase or decrease in food consumption. Both over and undereating can be signs of depression, so if you notice a change in either direction, you may want to consider your overall mental state. You will also want to track your behaviors in order to make sure you aren't doing anything that could be considered a risky behavior. This could be obvious things such as taking up an interest in dangerous activities, or it could be something subtler, like an increase in consumption of drugs or alcohol. Either way, it represents an underlying desire to deal with the problems you are experiencing that is manifesting in the worst way possible. If you fail to reign in these types of issues soon, they can easily lead to long-lasting harm.

If, based on the above or your own personal experiences, you believe that you are dealing with depression, then it is extremely important that you remain ever vigilant when it comes to warding off suicidal thoughts. If you have even one thought that involves seriously considering self-harm or even suicide, then you should contact emergency services right away or call the Suicide Prevention Hotline as this can be a dangerous issue to attempt to deal with on your own. Regardless of how you feel in the moment, it is crucial that you keep in mind that things can get better and that there is help out there. All you need to do is look for it.

Phobias

Much like with anxiety and depression, feeling afraid from time to time is a perfectly natural experience. While fear in moderation is useful when it comes to keeping us alive and alert, a phobia extends that fear out in intense ways that are impossible to control. When experiencing a normal fear response, it is common to feel uncomfortable when you are around whatever it is that you are afraid of. For example, if you were afraid of air travel then the thought of being on an airplane might cause you to break out in a cold sweat, and being on an airplane might not be fun, but you could power through if flying was required.

If you had a phobia of flying, however, then it is unlikely you could even make it onto the airplane without a serious dose of tranquilizers, and even then, it still might not be something that you could manage on your own. Those with phobias will go to extreme lengths to avoid the thing that they are afraid of, which is why their fear can be so difficult to deal with on a regular basis. If you feel as though the thing you are afraid of could literally appear at any time, it can be difficult, if not impossible, to carry out many otherwise common tasks.

In addition to the severity of the fear in question, if you have reason to assume that you are suffering from a phobia, then you are going to want to consider where it came from in the first place. This will likely be where your CBT therapy should begin. If you are only afraid of something, then you likely won't need to worry about the source of the fear, except when you are being confronted by it directly. If you have a phobia, however, then you are likely afraid of the fear you feel as much as you are of the thing that triggers your phobia in the first place.

Those with a serious phobia often find themselves living in fear of anything and everything that is going to trigger an extreme panic response, often going so far as to alter every other part of their life in an effort to find a situation where they can exist in a more relaxed state. If they know they are going to have to come up against a potential trigger, it is likely all they can think about, and it is something that they dwell on well past the point of reason. They will also likely find that they have a hard time sleeping through the night, and when faced with their phobia, they find it consumes their thoughts completely.

Chapter 9 Goal Setting

A lot of people know instantly what they would like to change in their lives and anyone can probably relate to this. People are very good at recognizing what needs to be done and what needs to be changed, but following through and implementing is easier said than done. The reasons for this can be numerous and it might be because the goal is so large and overwhelming to the point that people don't know where to start.

Luckily for everyone dealing with this, there are strategies which can make achieving goals and maintaining motivation so much easier. Everyone can benefit from setting a goal since when you have a goal, your motivation and confidence are higher and life is more interesting. Knowing how to set goals properly can allow you to improve the financial situation, catch up with old friends, save money, start a new hobby etc.

Knowing how to set goals also helps with the certain issue of the emotional and behavioral kind and that is why goal setting can be an important component of CBT. If someone is depressed because they are lonely then there is a good chance that setting a goal of improving relationships can help that person feel better. CBT frequently utilizes goal setting as a strategy and this can be really useful for people who find it hard to actually achieve goals once they are set.

The general approach for setting goals that is used as a component of CBT is as follows. First, a worthwhile goal has to be recognized and nothing can be done before that is identified. After a goal is set, then it is necessary to figure out how to get started based on the current circumstances and situation. After you know how to get started, then it is necessary to figure out step by step plan. It is better to have more small steps instead of having fewer large steps and this is actually known as chunking and the brain actually prefers this approach. You want to keep chunking until it doesn't make sense to make steps smaller. Steps should be small since that will be easier to follow. Accomplishing even the small steps will give you a bit of motivation which will keep pushing you forward and that is because frequent rewards work really well. By working this way, it is actually possible to overshoot and to do a bit more and it is a great feeling when you do so.

Whenever you feel disoriented, you can just ask yourself about what is the next step in order to continue with the process. Don't worry about the following steps, just stick to the current step and be in the now. Before you get started, you should also put some thought into what could go wrong so that you can deal with it swiftly if it occurs, so that you wouldn't stop for too long since that brings you out of the flow. You will never be able to predict all the possible roadblocks and it is better to do things imperfectly instead of not doing them at all. After you have a reasonable expectation about the possible obstacles, then you can take the first step.

If you just follow the goal achievement process described and the steps that you lay out in front of yourself, you will be accomplishing your goals and the confidence from that is just great. When setting out goals, you should also remember the ever popular SMART acronym for goal setting. This means that your goals have to be specific, measurable, achievable, relevant and timely.

Specific means that it is very clear what has to be done in order to achieve the goal. It shouldn't be vague since that is the opposite of specific. „Eat healthier" is vague, while „eat vegetables during one meal per day" is specific.

Goals have to be measurable and when they are measurable, then it is possible to track progress. For example, exercising 30 minutes 4 times per week is measurable and it is very easy to determine if that goal was accomplished or not.

The goal has to be achievable and it should be within your abilities at the moment.

The goal has to be relevant and it should have some meaning to you since this is how you will stay motivated. Wanting to make more money is good, but it is even better if you need that money for something such as traveling or donating to charity.

And finally, the goal has to be timely and that means that you should be instantly able to start working on that goal and you should also determine some deadline and a timeframe since that will give you a sense of urgency and focus. A good example of this is wanting to finish writing a book by the end of the year.

When you go after your goals in this way, it should all go smoothly and if you are having trouble with a certain step, then you should reassess your plan. Maybe the step has to be chunked. Look at every SMART component and change what you have to. Goal setting is a skill and you need to put in the time to get better at it, but it is a skill that is very valuable once you have it and it will help you get things done and to stop avoiding things.

Chapter 10 Understanding thoughts, feelings, and behaviors

Now that your goals are set, you are ready to move on to identifying those pesky negative thought patterns that were described in In learning to identify these, you are making it clear that you are dedicated to overriding the negativity that has been poisoning your mind for far too long. You will learn how to take over those negative thought patterns and challenge them into something more productive, and in the process of doing so, you ensure that you are thinking healthily, encouraging healthier behaviors in the process.

Negative Thought Patterns

Negative thought patterns have already been briefly touched upon, but as a brief recap, these are thoughts that are negative or distorted in some way—they are not productive, nor are they useful or helpful in any way. They simply exist to cause problems, and because they often develop and reside in the unconscious mind, you likely do not even know you have them in the first place. They hide beneath your awareness, pulling your strings and skewing how you act without actually ever being seen. They use you as a puppet, and in doing so, you may inadvertently push everyone you care about away from you, discouraging the relationships that you wish to foster and develop simply because no one wants to put up with the negativity you bring to the table.

When you have these thoughts, you likely realize that you always see the worst in things, but you may not realize the reason for that. You may not recognize that the reason you have those feelings of negativity is the negative thoughts lingering in the background. The easiest way to overcome this, then, is to make it a point to identify and challenge any negative thought that has been allowed to run your life for far too long.

Common Negative Thought Patterns

Before we begin the process of identifying the negative thought patterns you may have, you should start by learning to recognize what the 15 most common negative thought patterns are. These thought patterns are either cognitive distortions, meaning they are thoughts that are patently false in some way, or they are simply negative and unproductive in general, and therefore, should be avoided at all costs. These 15 thought processes are largely unconscious, but as soon as you learn to identify them, you are more likely to see them cropping up where you may least expect it.

Filtering

When you are engaging in filtering, you are focusing so much on the negative that you fail to see the positive. This is a common one in depression—you are willing to throw out the entire cake because one part cracked or crumbled, rather than seeing that it is still edible and delicious. You are likely to see the flaws as all-consuming, failing to recognize the fact that some things can have a flaw but still be largely positive and enjoyable.

Polarized thinking

When you fall for polarized thinking, like with filtering, you see things as good or bad. They are black or white, and there is no room for grey between them. You refuse to see that things can be more complicated than being perfect or an utter failure, entirely missing the fact that the middle ground there is the fact that people are likely to be average at whatever they attempt. After all, it is an average for a reason. Things do not have to be perfect in order to be acceptable or enjoyable, yourself included.

Overgeneralization

When you overgeneralize, you are making an assumption about what is happening around you based on a ridiculously small sample size. Similarly, you would probably reject any political statistic that says that a certain politician has a 93% approval rate. Why? Because you know that the entire sample was taken from one of that particular politician's allies and because you know it would be skewed and not representative of the general population. You should not be able to take something small, like a single instance in which a Chihuahua nipped at your heel to mean that all dogs are awful and should be avoided.

Jumping to conclusions

Also known as predicting the future, this is what you do when you assume you know how the story ends even though you have no concrete proof that that is, in fact, the way things will go. For example, you may assume that your partner will break up with you because all past partners have broken up with you, even if your partner is perfectly content sitting next to you on the couch at that particular moment.

Worst case scenario

When you focus on the worst possible result for something, you are engaging in worst-case scenario thinking. You are assuming the worst without any proof of it. For example, when your best friend's plane is delayed, you assume that the airport must have been taken a hostage and that someone is hijacking planes, even though there was no evidence that that was the case, and there is nothing on the news stating that it happened.

Personalization

When you engage in personalization, you make everything your problem and your fault. You assume that you have made your neighbor have a bad day, or that you are the cause of the cashier seeming depressed when he checks you out. You are directly responsible for every negative thing that happens around you when you engage in this kind of thinking.

Control fallacy

When you fall for this, you are blaming yourself for anything that happens. Similar to personalization, you assume that you are the root cause for everything, giving you control over what is happening around you.

Conversely, you may decide that you have nothing to do with whatever has happened, rejecting the possibility that you may have done something wrong when you feel the need to avoid accountability.

Fairness fallacy

Sometimes, you feel like things are not fair, and therefore, you refuse to accept them. That is the fairness fallacy—you assume that everything has to be fair because fair is right. Unfortunately, once you are out of early childhood, nothing is fair. Nothing in life is free or fair, and you have to earn what you want, regardless of what your neighbor, sibling, or friend has.

Blame

When blame is a problem for you, you constantly push blame on other people instead of accepting any real accountability. You would rather see the problem as being someone else instead of yourself, and will even blame something like the way the sun shone, or even blaming that the road was too slippery or the other person driving was too erratic if you rear-ended someone. Whatever the problem, it was not you, and you refuse to accept that it might have been.

"Shoulds"

When you focus on what something should have been instead of what it actually is, you are failing to see the world for what it really is. You are intentionally distorting your view of reality to fit your own preferences instead of attempting to acknowledge reality for what it is. You get so caught up in what should have happened that you fail to move forward when it does, in fact, fail to go how you expected it to.

Emotional reasoning

This is essentially deciding that something you are feeling is a fact. It usually goes hand-in-hand with labeling, which you will meet shortly. When you engage in emotional reasoning, you decide that you are feeling stupid; therefore, you are stupid. You allow your emotions to be the only justification you need to assign a value or label to something else, despite how unreliable emotions really are as judges.

Change fallacy

When you engage in this fallacy, you assume that everyone else will change to be what you want or need on a whim instead of recognizing people as individuals, and when that fails to happen, you get caught up in shock and being unwilling to accept what has happened.

Labeling

This is when you put a value or name on something without any real evidence. For example, when you decided to label yourself as stupid, as mentioned in emotional reasoning. You may also call someone dishonest because you are convinced that the other person has lied to you, or worthless because something failed. The label that is assigned does nothing to better the situation or help at all, and rather really just adds a name to something that is not going to make the situation or thing any more productive.

Refusal to admit wrong

This negative thought pattern involves refusing any accountability and stubbornly insisting you are right, even when the evidence showing otherwise is right in front of you. If someone tells you that you are wrong and provides you with the evidence that directly contradicts you, for example, you will vehemently deny it, insisting that you are right, even if you have to distort or lie about the subject in order to prove your point. You simply cannot be wrong about anything.

Heaven's reward

This last negative thought pattern is the belief that you are entitled to some sort of reward simply for doing the right thing. You assume that by doing something good, you deserve some sort of karma or reward or other instant gratification that will get you the result you are seeking out. You assume that good deeds are always rewarded, despite the fact that largely, that is not the case.

Identifying Negative Thought Patterns

With your newfound understanding of negative thought patterns that commonly arise, you are ready to begin identifying them. This is done largely through the same method that involved identifying problematic behaviors. However, instead of stopping at the behavior, you would continue to analyze what you are doing until you get down to the belief behind the behavior. You are essentially tracking the belief down further than you thought you could.

For example, imagine that you got angry because you felt like your partner wanted to leave you for someone else. You had no real evidence to support that thought, but have been entirely convinced it was true. You then acted as such, snapping at your partner, leading to a fight. After the fact, you decide that you want to figure out why that was a problem, to begin with, and you ask yourself why you felt that way. Perhaps the answer is that people always leave you in the end, seeking out someone else. Why is that relevant to you, you ask yourself once more. Your answer is that you are too worthless to be valuable in a relationship. Again, you ask why. The answer to that is that you are incapable of doing anything right, and suddenly, you have arrived at an automatic thought.

Automatic thoughts are those that you have entirely unconsciously, guiding your behavior without you needing to do anything to trigger them. They are behind-the-scenes, changing your assumptions and behaviors without your input, and you oftentimes do as they demand simply because you do not know they are there or problematic in the first place.

With that automatic thought identified, you must now take it and run it past the list of the 15 most common cognitive distortions and negative thought patterns in order to figure out if it fits the bill for any of them. So now, you have your automatic thought of, "I am not capable of doing anything right." Write that thought down and line it up against the negative thoughts. Right off the bat, you may notice at least three that it falls under—it fits the bill for filtering, polarized thinking, and overgeneralizing. It is arguably also a jump to conclusions.

You are filtering—you only focus on the negative. Surely, not every literal thing you have ever done has been wrong or failed. After all, you are still alive and breathing—that is something that you have done right! You eat, so you are able to do that right. You are reading this book right now, so you do not fail at reading. There are a few basic things you are doing right at this particular moment.

You are engaging in polarized thinking—you are either right or wrong with no in-between. Because you are not perfect, you assume that you are an utter failure, despite the fact that you have almost definitely done several things right and even well throughout your life.

You are engaging in overgeneralizing—you took a few key occurrences and turned them into a larger picture. Suddenly, you are never right or able to do something right, even though that is not the case. You took the handful of failures, which definitely do stand out in your mind because we, as humans, tend to remember the negative more than the positive as a survival mechanism—after all, when you remember what not to do when you make a mistake, you are not likely to repeat said mistake, which could have some very dangerous repercussions.

Lastly, you are engaging in jumping to conclusions—you assume that because you messed up in the past, you will never be able to do anything right. While admittedly, you will do something wrong again in the future because you are human and imperfect by nature, you cannot guarantee that every single thing you do from this moment on will be wrong.

Challenging Negative Thought Patterns

Once you have those negative thoughts decided upon and identified, it is time to begin challenging them. In challenging these negative thought patterns, you are able to better able to control them as they occur. When you realize that something you are doing is a direct result of some negative thoughts you are having, you suddenly have the ability to challenge them. After all, you cannot consciously challenge something that you were unaware of moments ago.

When you are attempting to challenge these negative thoughts, you are essentially stopping it in its tracks, questioning it, and then proving how it is wrong. Easier said than done, of course, but it is a valid way to challenge the thought. Ultimately, there are several questions that you can ask yourself directly in order to challenge any of the negative thoughts you are having.

As you challenge these thoughts, you are making it clearer to yourself that they are untrue or unproductive for some reason. In doing so and making these thoughts weaker or faultier, you are able to set them up for replacement in the future, something that CBT seeks to do. For example, imagine that you work as a barista. Someone comes in with a scowl on his face and barks an order at you. You do your best to follow, but you feel really self-conscious, thinking that it is your fault he is in a bad mood. You give him the coffee, and he takes a drink before slamming it down, declaring it is inedible, and then demanding a replacement drink. Confused because you followed the recipe, you make a new one, wondering if you did, in fact, mess it up and make the day worse for the guy.

You make the new drink and give it to him, and he leaves without tipping, and you are left feeling self-conscious, upset, and worthless in general.

You first go through the process of identifying the negative thought, pointing out that it is your own worthlessness and that your worthlessness is problematic for other people as well. You then compare it to your list of cognitive distortions and negative thought patterns and identify it as being patently false— you are personalizing and labeling yourself. Lastly, you must challenge the thought to really help yourself go away.

The way to do so involves taking a look at the following list of questions, asking yourself each:

Was your thought a negative thought fallacy?

Can you prove the thought as true?

Are you mixing up facts and opinions?

How would you advise a friend with the same thoughts and concerns as you have?

Can you be certain that what you think is true?

Is this such an important thought that you are willing to sacrifice your happiness to uphold it?

What is the worst-case scenario if your thought is true?

Can you cope with whatever the thought is? If so, how?

Is this emotional reasoning?

As you go through these questions, you will begin to see the truth—that the cognitive distortion is not, in fact, as important as you have made it out to be, and it can be forgotten about relatively easily. In challenging it and making it clear to yourself that it is illegitimate, you take away the power the thought had over you, to begin with, enabling yourself to move past it.

Why Some People Are More Prone to Depression Than Others

According to surveys, about 7% of the population experiences depression. With 7 billion people on the planet, that means 490 million people battle depression every year. Women are more likely to develop depression than men. In fact, about one and a half to three times more likely.

Why do you think that happens? Could it be attributed to the impossible standards that Society sets upon women? Could it be that females worry more about the house and caring for the family and putting their own needs ahead? Men experience stress just as much as women do but they are taught to keep their emotions inside and not show it.

Are we more depressed as a society that we were 50 years ago? Or is it that we are learning how to talk about it now as to where our parents and grandparents weren't? It wasn't something you did back in the day to discuss your feelings. Many times people dealt with their problems and depression behind closed doors. Now we have services to help us express ourselves, but it seems like we're becoming more depressed.

People don't have the same reactions when it pertains to stress and depression but there are several factors that do affect and cause depression. It may be a combination of two or more of the following factors that induce depression:

Neurotransmitter Defects

Neurotransmitters are mood-regulating chemicals in your body. Research says that it plays an important role as when these chemicals change in function and effect, it leads to depression.

Genetics

Unlike other genetic diseases such as Huntington's chorea or cystic fibrosis, depression doesn't seem to have an exact explanation or link why it exists on a person with a family history of depression.

Even if your family has a genetic predisposition towards depression, it doesn't guarantee that you will automatically have it, although there may be a possibility that you are prone to it as it also includes other factors as well.

Hormones

You have more possibilities of depression if you are susceptible to hormonal changes or imbalance. People who undergo hormonal changes like women who gave birth to children or those who have certain thyroid conditions experience symptoms of depression.

Abuse and Early Trauma Those who have experienced trauma and abuse in their early part of life are more prone to depression during their prime years or later part of their life.

Prescription Medication

Are you taking prescribed medications? Medicines such as sleeping pills, corticosteroids, Accutane, and interferon-alpha increase risks for depression.

Drug Abuse

It may be hard to determine why some people use drugs. It may be because they want to treat their depression by starting up with self-medication or they had previously started using drugs abusively. It's the same with prescription drugs. Certain illegal drugs can also cause you to have depression symptoms and its effects are seen.

Pain and Illnesses

There are two main reasons why pain and illnesses are related to depression.   The illness itself causes biochemical changes in the body that causes depression.

People with illnesses tend to be depressed as they experience prolonged pain, normal body function is limited or incapable and sometimes facing the possibility of death. They become depressed because of their health.

Death and Loss

Don't be surprised if you see somebody depressed after experiencing extreme losses whether it is in finances, properties or even lives of their loved ones. These events may have triggered their tendencies of depression.

Personality

Check this out if you've got some of these traits on your personality.

Overly dependent on others

Low self-esteem

Self-critical

Pessimism

If you have any of these traits, you are more prone to getting depressed.

Interpersonal Conflict

Family and friend conflicts also contribute to increased stress. Undergoing conflicts such as these will tend you to develop depression.

Stress

You can have stress whether your life is uphill (getting married) or downhill (losing your job). When you are under attack by stress, your cortisol levels rise to the point that possibly affects the transmission of serotonin, a mood-regulating molecule.

In other words, depression is a complicated situation wherein certain factors are involved, e.g. biologically based differences in brain function. The more you are faced with various factors, the more tendencies and possibilities to develop depression.

Chapter 11 Secrets of Developing the Best Attitude

Many studies have found that your attitude makes the difference between achieving success and becoming a failure. You might be a very qualified individual, but if your attitude is nasty, you will end up achieving less than an underqualified person with a great attitude. In many fields of work, success is down to the collaborative skills of individuals, and if you have a poor attitude, you will make a poor teammate.

A negative attitude is a psychological impediment to success, but even worse, it makes people shun you. If you have a terrible attitude, you are going to have a terrible time of it. Thankfully, your poor attitude is not set in stone. You can change it if you choose to.

The following are some of the secrets of developing a warm attitude that will draw people in and also open you up to opportunities:

Stop Acting Entitled

When you act entitled, you send the message that you have too high an opinion of yourself. This will antagonize other people, and you will have zero allies. When you are on good terms with people, you have the best environment for cultivating a great attitude.

Be Grateful

If someone shows you kindness, the least you can do is appreciate their effort. People notice those who never appreciate their kind gestures. It reeks of entitlement. Be grateful in small and big things alike. It will help you establish connections and enter into mutually beneficial relationships.

Improve Your Lifestyle

Your lifestyle has a great influence on the person you end up becoming. If you're into binge drinking and spending your weekends laughing around with female or male hookers, it would be quite challenging to develop a great attitude. A great attitude goes together with a certain awareness of a moral compass. So, cut out the drunken weekends, and channel that time into spending time with your loved ones. Another important aspect of your lifestyle is your diet. Cut out the junk and start preparing healthy meals. Healthy meals are not only good for your emotional and mental health but also your wallet.

Reframe Your Challenges

Regardless of the challenges that you might be facing, never assume a rigid approach. Look at your challenges from various angles. The more flexible you are, the more creativity you stir in yourself, and ultimately, you will be in a far better position to solve your challenges.

Embrace Rejection

Harden your heart a little bit so that rejection won't cripple you. The fact of the matter is that on the path to reaching your goals, you are going to get rejected more times than you will care to remember. Read about movie stars and the rejection that they go through. When you learn to embrace rejection, you elevate yourself into the mindset of an unstoppable winner.

Use Positive Words

If you have a negative attitude, it follows that negative words will escape your mouth when describing your life. You will always come from a perspective of lack and misery. Change this pattern by starting to say positive things about yourself. Look at your glass as half full – not half empty.

Become a Doer

Instead of talking about the grand plans that you haven't acted upon yet, make a rule of talking about the things you have actually done. This will push you into becoming more of a doer than merely a talker. For instance, instead of saying, "I'll drop my CV to twenty offices this week," it should be, "This week, I dropped my CV to twenty offices."

Become Wary of Energy Vampires

Sadly, not everyone in your life is well-meaning. Various people act like a vampire – they drain your energy. When you discover an energy vampire, you want to pull away from them as quickly as you can, so that they don't deplete your positive energy.

Deep Breathing Exercise

There is a direct relationship between our breathing and our emotions. When we are constricted and have trouble breathing, we become susceptible to negativity. However, when we inhale oxygen-rich air on the regular, we tend to become grounded. Practice deep-breathing exercises and watch your negative thinking patterns fade away.

Choose to See the Positive Side

No matter how bleak the situation appears, always choose to see the brighter side of things. If your company posts losses, don't wallow in despair but choose to see it as an opportunity to prove your mettle. If your company posts massive profits next year, you will reclaim your top spot, and inspire others. Always choose to see the bright side of things.

Be More of a Problem-Solver

A negative person points out problems for the sake of tearing things down. They rejoice in bringing people down to their level. But you should place as much thought into the solution as you place into the problem. Instead of criticizing and leaving it at that, offer a solution, and the other party will appreciate your criticism.

Become the Agent of Joy

There is no shortage of sadists in the world. However, there aren't enough people to spread joy, which is what we need more of. Become the agent of spreading joy around the world. When you have a positive impact on the lives of people, it increases your self-esteem and challenges your natural selfish tendencies.

Cultivate Meaningful Relationships

When you're in a relationship, you learn to become a giver, not always a taker. Being selfless is a vital element of a positive attitude. As a giver, you operate from the mindset of abundance, and this leads you to become a resourceful person.

Develop Crisis Management Skills

Whatever happens is not the actual problem, but your reaction is where the problem is. You cannot escape crises for as long as you are alive. However, if you have crisis management skills, you are far more likely to emerge out of the situation unscathed, and yet preserve your good image.

Chapter 12 A-B-C (Antecedence - Belief - Consequence)

Significant to Cognitive Behavior Therapy is the ABC Technique of Irrational Beliefs. Using this tool can aid the therapist in analyzing the process leading to the development of irrational beliefs in a person. This may be recorded in a three-column table.

A – Antecedent (Activating Events or Object Situation)

This is the first column where the objective situation is logged. It states the event that creates a high-emotional response or develops negative dysfunctional thinking.

This actually refers to the environment or the event preceding the target behavior or behavior of interest which is being analyzed in the treatment. The antecedent essentially provides the trigger to a certain behavior.

Anything can be an antecedent. It could be a comment of another person in the presence of others. Changes of environment can likewise be a common antecedent.

B - Beliefs

This is a record of all negative thoughts that occur which relates to the event or situation.

C - Consequences

This is the record of all negative feelings and dysfunctional behaviors which occurred afterward following those listed in column two.

While those mentioned in the second column are viewed as the link between the situation and the distressing emotions, items on the third column are explained as emotions or negative thoughts which the person thinks are caused by A. This could be sorrow, anxiety, anger, etc.

In Applied Behavior Analysis, these 3 elements - antecedent, behavior, and consequence provide what are considered the building blocks in understanding, analyzing, and the potential to change one's behavior or action. Analyzing behavior via the ABC model is included in a comprehensive functional assessment of behavior.

A is action. B is belief. C is consequence. So when something happens in your life typically something traumatic were the very least memorable, you develop a belief from that experience. You hold on to that and assume that that is your reality. As a result, you live out the consequences of that belief, abiding by and falling in line with that belief.

For example, remember a time when you were in high school and a friend passed by. You said "hello". She didn't respond nor return the greeting. Instead, she continued walking past you without acknowledging your presence. The thought that might then popped up in your head is that maybe she didn't like you. The emotional feelings you would have then would be the feeling of rejection and maybe sadness.

Physically, you may have felt pain in your heart or a prick on your ego. Your next action would be to avoid her next time. You may even make it a point not to speak to her on purpose when you did see her.

That's just one example to illustrate the situation. If you go to a therapist they might be able to help you break it down to identify the thought process that led you to your current situation.

But what if the situation is like this? You're walking down the hallway and you're having a bad day as you walked past your friend she ignored you. Maybe you were then thinking she's not in a good mood and her ignoring you wasn't intentional or maybe she was just caught up in her own thoughts. Then you start to wonder if she's all right.

The emotional feeling of being hurt or even angry in you could have changed. When before you believed that you might feel rejected and was angry to think that your friend had neglected you. The next action would be to call her after school to see if she's okay. Can you see how these two scenarios are different?

All of these come down to how you think and see the world around you. Cognitive behavioral therapy helps you evaluate different thought processes and ideas based on what you see and how you interpret those situations in a completely different way. This is really good news because perception is a reality and if we can start to analyze the way we perceive things and make a change, we will find that our lives will begin to improve just by the way we perceive the world around us.

Chapter 13 In Cases When There Are Multiple Issues (Problem Behaviors) Or Antecedent Events

Composition of Cognitive Behavior Therapy

The thoughts and feelings you experience help reinforce your beliefs, whether faulty or not. This is why troubled behavior eventually affects different aspects of your life, such as academics, family, work, and personal relationships. If you are struggling with confidence, for example, you will always feel inadequate and not worthy of the chances that come your way. You do not believe in your appearance or your ability to perform the task required, and because of this negative thought process, you avoid any situation that might warrant interaction with your peers or anyone who can challenge you. In the process, you start passing up chances for advancing your progress or career at work or in school.

Your therapist will help you identify the problematic beliefs keeping you from realizing your potential. The procedure is called functional analysis. At this juncture, you are both learning the impact that your situations, feelings, and thought process have on maladaptive behavior. Functional analysis might be difficult, especially if you have been dealing with introspection. However, if you work through it, functional analysis lays the perfect foundation for insight, reflection, and rediscovering yourself, which are essential in your healing process.

After functional analysis, your therapist will advance you to a behavioral approach. In this stage, they try to understand the behaviors that trigger the problem you are dealing with. You will also learn new skills applicable in real life, which will help you manage your situation better.

In a behavioral approach, consider someone battling drug addiction. You learn new skills to cope with your daily life and must rehearse these skills frequently. These skills come in handy if you find yourself in a situation that might encourage a relapse.

CBT is a step-by-step process toward positive behavioral change. You will learn how to handle yourself in a situation that might provoke the behavioral challenges you are facing. After this, you learn how to communicate with the people around you—your family, friends, workmates, and acquaintances. The people in your immediate environment play a significant role in your progress. They also help you achieve your therapy goals faster and help you feel less isolated.

Lessons from CBT

CBT is about imparting useful learning and coping skills, which will help you manage when faced with challenging situations. There are many ways of coping, and your therapist will help you figure out what works for you. One thing you will learn to overcome is avoidance.

You will learn pain management techniques. Pain is a normal part of life that we experience at different times and must work through. By avoiding your pain or situations you are uncomfortable with, you increase your fear. Through CBT, you will learn how to confront your worst fears. Confrontation is a manageable and gradual process, and in the end, you will have more faith in your ability to overcome your adversities.

CBT also teaches you how to explore your thoughts and desires. By writing things down, you have the chance to take a different perspective. You reflect on the notes you make, and this should help you learn how to change the negativity you have been feeling.

At the end of your CBT sessions, you should have also learned how to relate better to other people. If you make assumptions about them or their motivations, you will learn how to give them the benefit of the doubt, as you would expect them to do for you. Instead of always assuming the worst about people, you take a rational perspective of your interactions.

What if CBT Fails?

While CBT has proven to be successful for many people, not everyone gets as much help as they hope for. If at the end of your CBT sessions you see little or no progress, make this known to your therapist. You do not have to wait until the sessions are over.

CBT is about honesty, and you should be open about your perception of the sessions. Your therapist can also help you find ways to make the sessions better so you can get more out of them. If things do not work out, you can consider getting a different therapist. Even the most experienced cognitive therapists have difficulty with some patients (Beck, 2011).

If you do not strike a bond with your therapist, it might not be easy to open up. You will hold back on the things you feel are too dear to you. By shutting out your therapist, you will be placing stumbling blocks on your way to success.

Risks Associated with CBT

While there is minimal emotional risk linked to CBT, dealing with painful experiences and feelings is not easy, and this in itself can be a source of stress for you. Treatment in most cases means you must face circumstances you have been comfortable avoiding for a long time. However, you must understand that the goal of CBT is to help you learn to deal with the stress and anxiety that comes with facing your fears and dealing with them constructively and safely.

Chapter 14 Identify And Break Negative Thinking Patterns

During the course of your day, you have more automatic thoughts than you can imagine. These can range from noticing someone's shirt color to registering when a person decides to merge into your lane while driving and you instinctively slow just enough to give the driver enough space to pass you. These automatic thoughts are snap judgments that influence your behavior without taking up your conscious thought processes. By not having to focus on these instinctive behaviors, you are free to worry about more complicated thoughts that require more cognition instead, such as worrying about your work deadline or how you will schedule your evening.

These thoughts come unbidden but are quickly ignored or forgotten, as they are hardly relevant to continue about your day. You do not think about why you need to slow down when approaching a stop light, nor do you think about how you slow down; you simply do it and continue driving. These involuntary, reactionary thoughts are your automatic thoughts. They can be neutral or somewhere on the positive or negative scale.

While these thoughts are meant to be useful, sometimes, they can be skewed and become detrimental instead.

When automatic thoughts become detrimental, they are considered negative automatic thoughts. This is one of the types of thoughts that CBT seeks to correct. Negative automatic thoughts are also largely unconscious, and they color your perception of what is happening around you. These are underlying thoughts of unworthiness, uselessness, feeling as if you are unloved, or believing you are unimportant or unintelligent. These thoughts may have been internalized through past experiences, and they color your perception of everything. Any time something goes wrong, your automatic negative thought will feel justified. For example, if you take a wrong turn on your way to a new restaurant to meet someone, you might immediately tell yourself, "Wow, of course, I messed that up and missed my turn! I can't even follow my GPS right without messing something up. Now I'm late, and my friend is going to be angry." Things could have been just fine leading up to that moment, but as soon as you made a mistake, you beat yourself up over it.

That diatribe is an example of the behavior caused by an automatic negative thought. In that instance, the automatic negative thought was likely feelings of worthlessness or feeling unintelligent. The automatic negative thought is your automatic reaction of beating yourself up at any signs of perceived failure. The undertone to the thought is that you believe you are worthless, unintelligent, and unwanted. If you had told yourself, "I am stupid, and no one likes me," you would likely recognize that that is an incorrect statement, but that is the implication when you said what you did to yourself. These negative automatic thoughts can result in reacting in over-the-top fashions, such as screaming at a waiter who drops a cup, or breaking into tears because you accidentally forgot to message something silly and unimportant to a friend when you originally told her you would. CBT will teach you how to identify and correct these thoughts with a variety of different skills. For further instruction and information, see II: Strategy 6: Identifying and Challenging Negative Automatic Thoughts.

Cognitive Distortions

Like negative automatic thoughts, cognitive distortions are automatic thoughts, but they are distorted or patently false in some way, shape, or form. These are beliefs you may hold and take at face value, but something about them is inaccurate. Think of this like logic: If a logical argument is unsound, it is essentially worthless and can be discarded on the basis of being unsound. For example, the argument, "If I hop three times right now, then the volcano next to me will suddenly erupt. I hopped three times; therefore, the volcano is blowing up," is logically valid, meaning that the structure of the argument follows the logical rule pattern known as modus ponens. However, anyone can look at that argument and recognize that it is nonsense, even if it follows the pattern. Just as arguments can be unsound or unreasonable, so too can beliefs about the world.

These cognitive distortions can be anything from seeing your neighbor in a foul mood, and automatically deciding it is your fault. You somehow manage to rationalize the jump from point a to b, using cognitive distortions. Because your beliefs at their core are what is flawed, you have no issues accepting it quicker than you would accept the nonsense argument about hopping and volcanoes erupting. It fits the very logical pattern you have developed and fits into your argument, so you see no reason to give it a second thought or challenge it, even if it leaves you feeling down about yourself, anxious, or angry.

These cognitive distortions can be identified, though it does require time and effort. They typically follow specific patterns or fallacies, and because of that, if you analyze your deepest core beliefs, you will begin to be able to identify which of them have become distorted. This is another of the strategies that will be in II. See Strategy 3: Identifying and Challenging Cognitive Distortions for more information on how to identify cognitive distortions and begin to challenge them.

Cognitive Restructuring

Cognitive restructuring is the process of altering your way of thinking. CBT recognizes that thoughts, feelings, and actions are an endless cycle in which thoughts influence feelings, which influence actions, which in turn influence thoughts. Everything you do feeds into this endless cycle. CBT seeks to disrupt this cycle in order to change it. For example, imagine you are someone with an anger problem. You often think about things negatively, which keeps you in a negative mood, which causes you to lash out in anger, which only makes you think even more negatively about whatever triggered the outburst in the first place.

CBT interrupts one of those aspects, typically either thoughts or actions, which upsets the entire cycle. For example, if the cause of the angry outburst was that you disliked a restaurant that your family chose to go to for dinner, so you were already in a bad mood when you walked in the door, which contributed to your explosion, CBT would likely seek to change your negative thought. Instead of being annoyed at the restaurant, CBT would have you instead focus on the positive aspect of the event, such as going to dinner with your family and enjoying the occasion, even if the food is not your favorite. By focusing on enjoying your family, you are likely to be in a better mood, which will make you much less inclined to react explosively in anger. This cognitive restructuring is used a lot in challenging both negative automatic thoughts and cognitive distortions.

Core Beliefs

Core beliefs are the beliefs you hold about yourself. They can be either negative or positive, but they color every interaction you have with others and how you perceive the world around you. These core beliefs are largely unconscious, but they can be identified through plenty of introspection and self-reflection. These beliefs are typically developed over a long period of time, typically beginning in childhood, or through significant life events. These are typically rigid beliefs, and you will react according to them, even going so far as to unconsciously force what is happening around you to fit into the core beliefs while denying or disregarding anything that would contradict it.

For example, someone with depression may look at every negative interaction he has as a sign that he is unworthy of love, or he is worthless to everyone around him. However, he will be virtually blind to every instance of those who care about him going out of their way to show they care, such as sending him a silly text of a meme they say on the internet that they know he will appreciate or having his favorite food delivered to him on his birthday.

These core beliefs can be cognitive distortions or colored by negative automatic thoughts, and they are important to understand. Once you understand how you feel about yourself, you are able to decide whether you like how you feel. If you do, you know you are secure with yourself. If you do not, you can begin the steps of cognitive restructuring to alter them.

Emotional Triggers

Sometimes, something around us suddenly triggers an overwhelming sense of negative emotion. You could have been happily chatting with someone, and at the drop of a hat, suddenly felt your blood boiling, your pulse racing, and like you cannot decide between screaming at someone or punching them. This reaction is called being emotionally triggered. You may know during, or after the fact that your reaction is irrational and disproportionate, but despite that, you cannot control it. The best you can do is seek to understand what your emotional trigger is so you can plan a way to avoid blowing up in the future.

Emotional triggers are typically related to some sort of trauma that has caused you to internalize a strong reaction to things reminiscent of the trauma. Someone who suffered through an abusive relationship might be triggered by someone saying a common phrase if it was one the abusive partner said on a regular basis. Someone traumatized by a dog attack at a young age may be triggered by the sound of barking. Someone home from war may be triggered by loud sounds reminiscent of explosions or gunfire.

Understanding what your emotional triggers are will help you begin the process of cognitive restructuring in order to retrain yourself to be less reactive to them. If you are aware that you react negatively to people with beards that surprise you, there are methods you can use to desensitize yourself to them, so your reactions are not as strong or negative. Through a combination of cognitive restructuring and exposure to your trigger in a controlled environment, you will be able to overcome these emotional triggers and stop allowing them to rule your life.

Chapter 15 Discover 7 Inspiring Tales of CBT Success

There are many reasons to use cognitive behavioral therapy to help lower your overall stress or treat depression, general anxiety disorder, social anxiety disorder, obsessive-compulsive disorder, post-traumatic stress disorder, addiction, bipolar disorder, and more. However, if you have not yet experienced these benefits for yourself it can be hard to believe. Thankfully, there have been many people who have come before you. In this, we will look at some real-life stories of success gained due to CBT. Please keep in mind that the names have been changed to respect the patients' privacy.

Christine's Story

Christine felt different from everyone else around her. Of course, nobody else was like her, she was just being silly. Weak. Pathetic. That was her. Why couldn't she cope like everyone else? Everyone must get anxious from time to time, so why is it that she was the only one who was completely worthless?

At thirty-nine-years-old, she was married, in good health, and was holding down a responsible job. While she considered herself generally confident, friendly, and successful. Not only that, but she had a long track record of achieving whatever she set her mind to. She was determined to push herself and attain her goals. Yet, she held a life-long secret.

What was her secret that she didn't want anyone to know? She had been bullied. Both physically and emotionally. This past had caused its own scars, its own pain. However, the cruelest bully by far had not been a school mate, a neighbor, a family member, or anyone else she knew. The worst of the bullies resided within her own mind as a consequence of her nearly non-existent self-esteem.

The inner bully would constantly berate her, hurling insults that hit right at her insecurities: "You're an embarrassment," "You're ridiculous," "You're weird," "You're stupid," "Nobody likes you, they don't even love you," You're not good enough." These insults, and more, chipped away on her on a daily basis.

Then, one cold evening in the middle of winter, Christine was wandering alone on the beach. As the cold wind whipped her face it stung against the tears that fell from her eyes, as she felt dead inside, completely useless and numb. Life had not been easy lately. During the past several months, she had experienced a panic attack while on the job, which left her feeling completely ill at ease and unnerved. What if it happened again? However, she had been through the worst circumstances in life, couldn't she just cope?

Well, she tried to cope. But after a few weeks, she could no longer think straight. She became confused and forgetful. Unable to sleep at night she was in a constant state of panic, feeling out of control and emotionally raw. She could no longer keep up outward appearances, as she couldn't remember her pin number and would leave the keys in the front door to her apartment. Loud noises were jarring, she couldn't handle being around other people. A single conversation with a friend or colleague would send her into a state of uncontrolled paranoia. At one point, Christine even forgot where she lived and how to drive.

She had a complete breakdown.

At this point, she felt as though she was losing her mind. She knew it was no longer something she could cope with on her own, after all, coping wasn't happening. She went to her general practitioner completely distressed and overwhelmed, which resulted in being diagnosed with generalized anxiety disorder, given an anti-anxiety medicine prescription, and requiring two weeks off of work. With the help of the medication, Christine was able to cope until she got into a therapist, who set up a six-month cognitive behavioral therapy schedule for her.

Her therapist, who specialized in CBT, helped Christine to understand what was happening and why she felt so out of control. Not only that, but her therapist also helped her to finally develop an understanding of her inner critic which was a result of unreasonable and self-imposed rules that she unintentionally created for herself over a period of many years. These rules she had formed for herself all formed due to deeply held core beliefs, which were created through her interactions in the world. These beliefs formed her cognition.

However, Christine now learned that sometimes these core beliefs are flawed, skewed, harmful, or completely wrong. They form an irrational cognition. When exploring her cognition and the beliefs it held, Christine had enlightening experiences. Although, other times it was really upsetting, as these beliefs dealt with long-buried experienced and wounds that were raw and painful. Despite some of these situations being painful, it helped her to be able to discuss and reassess the inaccuracies, allowing her to create new and healthier thoughts in their place.

With her six months of CBT therapy, Christine was able to rediscover herself, her voice, and her presence at work. No longer was she worried about any possible error she might make, obsessing over past mistakes, or over-analyzing every small detail of everything that happened to her.

While she was previously obsessed with others' opinions of herself, causing her to panic, she has now learned too not to worry about it. Feeling so liberated as to even say "so what?!" if a person holds a negative opinion or wrong idea about her.

After now finishing her CBT, Christine has made remarkable progress, however, she is still working on overcoming decades of an irrational cognition. She is still working on accepting herself as being lovable, but she can now say "I'm alright." Social events still are a little challenging, yet she can now take compliments and positive feedback. No longer does she take everything personally. She has learned how to be open and share her heart with those around her. Instead of pretending everything is okay, she has learned when and how to ask for help.

Christine has even been open about sharing her mental health struggles with others, which have allowed them to better understand her. Moreover, this had led to more of her friends and coworkers sharing their own mental health struggles, allowing everyone to better support one another.

The difference before and after CBT is night and day, and Christine only continues to improve as she uses the tools and techniques she learned in therapy.

Sarah's Story

People were often shocked by the classic small-town feel of Sarah's hometown. Where she lived, everyone knew everybody else, no one locked their cars or even their homes, and every Friday night the whole town would go on down to the local high school to watch the football game. Growing up on a hobby farm right outside of town, she enjoyed life with her parents, who were the most generous and funny people she knew.

She was the happiest girl on earth. At least, she should have been. The truth was that there was something completely overtaking her life and stealing her joy. What was that? Undiagnosed obsessive-compulsive disorder, or OCD.

For twenty years, Sarah tried numerous failed prescriptions, experienced side effect after side effect from the list of medications and participated in countless hours of talk therapy. Her psychiatrist didn't know what else to do. Finally, after nothing else had worked, she was referred to the city to see an OCD specialist. This specialist was going to change her life, as he asked her if she wanted to try cognitive-behavioral therapy.

However, he said, "It will be hell."

While her new OCD specialist knew that the therapy process wouldn't be easy for someone like Sarah (who was suffering from severe OCD), he believed it would be worth it. It was important that he was upfront with her so that she was prepared to get through the hard times and see the sun rise over the horizon when things started to improve.

Sarah was willing to do it. After all, daily life with OCD was already hell. She was willing to endure short-term discomfort if it meant finally getting her severe symptoms managed after over twenty years. She finally had a glimmer of hope, and she was willing to see it through.

During her first couple of weeks with her new therapist, they mostly dealt with explaining the process and going through her condition. To this end, she was asked about her specific compulsions and obsessions and what triggered them. The purpose of this was so that her therapist could later on work on using CBT-based exposure therapy. After all, he couldn't push her buttons and to trigger her compulsions if he didn't first understand them. For instance, he would say "How much would it stress you out if you couldn't [insert compulsion] after [insert trigger] happened?" While she knew answering these questions would make life difficult for a short time, she was all in and laid all her cards out on the table.

This was her last hope for a happy and normal life.

Sarah's therapist had her complete the Yale-Brown Obsessive-Compulsive Scale, which is a test that psychology professionals use to not only diagnose OCD, but also to determine what treatment is needed. Thanks to this scale, Sarah was able to learn that her case is moderate. This surprised her since it had ruined so much of her life. Although, there are people who experience this disorder to such a degree that they are unable to touch their loved ones, can't leave home, and wash their hands with pure bleach and Brillo pads.

The therapist helped her to create measurable goals for her initial treatment plan. The main two goals were:

- A fifty-percent distress reduction when focused on upsetting stimulus

- Six consecutive weeks of no rituals or avoidance

The next few months of therapy were beginning to sound very, very long.

Sarah's form of OCD is known as scrupulosity, meaning most of her obsessions were religion-based. For instance, this dealt with a fear of blasphemy and being condemned to hell.

Obviously, she could not be literally exposed to hell, which meant that most of her exposure therapy was imaginative. For this to happen, her therapist would begin to write a story and then it was Sarah's homework to finish the story. This story took place in the worst day she could imagine, quite literally as the story ended up taking place in hell.

After Sarah completed the story, her therapist would add his own additions to it and then record it digitally on audio. It was then Sarah's homework to listen to this eighteen-minute recording four times daily, and without acting on any of her compulsions. When listening to this, she had to record her anxiety levels when prompted. She would continue doing this until her anxiety to the audio was reduced by fifty percent from her initial reaction.

It was terrible.

Exposing herself to that recording was like torture. Her OCD was constantly being triggered, yet she wasn't allowed to do anything that would help to ease the anxiety. It made her heart race and left her sick to her stomach. She was terrified. She hated it.

While Sarah was supposed to listen to the audio four times a day, she was supposed to do it in two sittings. This means that because it is an eighteen-minute audio recording she would have to spend thirty-six minute at a time, twice a day, exposing herself to her triggers. At first, she would try to start out her morning listening to half of her audio for the day. However, before long she could no longer do this. It became overwhelming to start off her day miserable. The weight of this pressing on her first thing in the morning made it difficult to even get out of bed. Therefore, she had to switch things up and instead begin doing her exposure therapy later in the day. This helped her to no longer dread waking up.

CBT with a focus on exposure therapy felt like needless torture before long. After eight or nine weeks when nothing felt like it was improving, Sarah wanted to quit. She was frustrated, largely with her therapist, as she felt absolutely certain she couldn't accomplish what he believed. However, when she was at her lowest her therapist helped to introduce her to a tool that helped. Instead of thinking the blasphemous thoughts directly for her exposure therapy, her therapist suggested she think, "My obsessive-compulsive disorder wants me to think [insert thought]." This was just what Sarah needed.

Within a week of introducing this tool that provided a way to side-step herself into exposure therapy, it began to click. One day while listening to the audio recording, what was previously a device of torture and terror, and instead she thought "This is so annoying." That was it, no terror. No torture. Simple annoyance. And then, she smiled, as she realized she finally made progress.

This was only part of her six-month-long CBT experience with exposure therapy, but it was one of the most memorable. For Sarah, this was one of the hardest things she's ever had to do, however, it was still easier than living for over twenty years with unmanaged OCD. Now, years later, she only wishes she had gone through the process sooner. For the first time, her life feels as if it is her own.

David's Story

David, in his late forties, realized he was suffering from debilitating depression in December of 2015. He knew he needed helped and took a leave from work. However, after eight months on the waiting schedule with the National Health Services, it was recommended by his general practitioner that he instead try going to his local Cognitive-Behavioral Therapy clinic.

While his depression had been devastating, from the very first appointment he saw a ray of light and knew that seeking CBT was the right choice. During every appointment, his therapist was a reassuring and calming presence, which helped him better deal with his own issues.

While David was previously feeling dread and despair without any answers, he was able to finally understand his own thoughts and feelings. Not only that, but he learned how these thoughts affected his behavior, giving him a path out of the darkness. He now has an understanding and deep insight into his cognition and the problems he developed over the years. David can now even recognize destructive patterns of thinking that were only worsening his depression, behavior, and emotions.

With CBT, David now has an arsenal of techniques and tools he can use to maintain his mental health. He knows questions he can use to challenge unbalanced thinking and how to now look at situations in a new light. Together with his therapist, he developed new strategies to help in his specific situation, which helps him to reduce his symptoms of depression and hopelessness.

Before long, David's self-esteem and confidence were better than ever before. No longer is he living every day of his life miserable, wondering what the point of living is. Not only has CBT helped him greatly, but because of his experience, he even recommended the process to two close friends, who have also benefited from the therapy.

Joy's Story

During her senior year of high school, Joy began to experience severe panic attacks. Every day when she tried going into the school she would be overcome and paralyzed with these attacks, making it difficult just to breathe.

In what should have been a year of shining experiences with her friends before leaving high school, instead she was suffering from her mental health. What triggered the change? The problem was multi-faceted. First, she had been forced to undergo her studies in an extremely hot classroom for several weeks, leading to fear of it causing her to become sick. Not only that, but some kids at her school had begun to bully her, completely shattering any confidence she had. No longer could she be in a large group or crowd of people without developing a panic attack.

Thankfully, a friend of Joy's mom had heard about cognitive behavioral therapy and recommended it to her. Almost immediately after meeting her new CBT specialized therapist, Joy made a connection with him. He was able to form a trusting bond with her, allowing her to feel comfortable despite her struggles from bullying.

After completing her CBT sessions and learning new techniques and tools for her anxiety and panic attacks, Joy is once again joyful. With help from her panic diary and other techniques, she can cope with any difficult situation that arises, giving her the confidence to once again return to high school. CBT was just what she needed, and now Joy is set on a path to success as she earns her high school diploma and gets ready to move into adulthood.

John's Story

After leaving an emotionally abusive relationship, John had developed Generalized Anxiety Disorder. This disorder can affect everyone differently and was affecting John in some rather scary ways. He didn't know what was happening. All of a sudden, it seemed like his life had plummeted. He constantly became overwhelmed with fear, worried that someone would overpower him and choke the air from his lungs. To prevent mistakenly feeling as if he was choking, he had to constantly chew on mints, so he could clearly feel the air entering and leaving his lungs.

Not only that, the anxiety was making it impossible for John to use public transport, leave home alone, or eat in restaurants.

Thankfully, John decided to see a CBT specialist. His therapist soon explained that he had to stop relying on the mints, as they were only worsening his anxiety. Thankfully, in place of the mints, he was given various CBT techniques and tools in order to cope and heal.

Finally, after a few weeks of therapy John's anxiety was beginning to improve. Before long, he was even able to leave the house alone again. He was able to enjoy going out for dinner with family and friends. John got his life back again, and it was all thanks to cognitive behavioral therapy.

Tony's Story

Tony lived with severe social anxiety disorder, which his partner always helped him cope with. However, after he and his partner separated, he was left with nobody else to turn to for help.

At first, Tony made the mistake of turning to alcohol as a coping mechanism and only socializing when he could drink. However, he soon learned that this wasn't the answer, and his anxiety only grew worse.

Once alcohol didn't work, Tony decided the only choice left was to isolate himself. This also didn't work, as he became incredibly depressed from the isolation. This led him to the realization that he could not get through this on his own, he needed someone to help him heal, increase his confidence, and get him back out in the world to socialize.

Tony ended up seeing a therapist who started him on a CBT treatment plan. With his weekly sessions, homework, and new-found techniques Tony was able to find his confidence for the first time, without relying on another person. By the end of therapy, he was able to experience such a stark decrease in anxiety that he had to confidence to attend a formal-dress party and regularly go out on his own without anyone to lean on.

The difference was night and day. For the first time, Tony could fully be himself.

Tabitha's Story

After struggling under the pressure of domestic violence, Tabitha had developed post-traumatic stress disorder. This would leave her awake at night shaking with nightmares. Even during the day, she wasn't free of the nightmares, as she would experience vivid flashbacks that placed her back at the hands of her abuser.

Constantly Tabitha was being overwhelmed with anxiety and panic. She couldn't trust a soul, as it felt as if danger was right around every corner, with everyone out to get her.

Before long, Tabitha's PTSD was so severe she was unable to leave the house, see anyone, or do anything except for caring for her young children. Increasingly her depression and anxiety both worsened as the situation continued and prescribed medication had no effect.

It wasn't easy for Tabitha to go to therapy, but it was well worth it. Her life is now back on track. She can finally socialize again. She found confidence, took up volunteering, and was even able to enter a new romantic relationship.

Tabitha has the life she never thought would be possible again. She can be unapologetically herself and be a better mom to her children.

Chapter 16 About Cognitive Behavioral Therapy

As you already know, this book is all about Cognitive Behavioral Therapy. While some of you may have heard of it, others may be completely unfamiliar with it. This is why it is important to first gain an understanding of the basic concept of this therapy. You will learn what it is and why people choose to use this particular therapy in the first place.

Cognitive Behavioral Therapy is a psychotherapeutic treatment that helps people manage their issues by understanding their thoughts and behavior and eventually changing them for the better. It helps you to take any thoughts and behaviors that are not benefiting you and replace them with ones that actually will benefit you.

A lot of research has shown that Cognitive Behavioral Therapy may be one of the most effective treatments for anxiety, depression, and other such disorders. It is mostly used to treat various disorders, including addictions, phobias, depression, and anxiety. This particular therapy has been known to surpass most other types of therapy with its effectiveness and its ability to treat people. However, you may not appreciate the power of Cognitive Behavioral Therapy until you see it in action. As you learn about it, you will see how reasonable this treatment approach is. Therapists admit that Cognitive Behavioral Therapy not only helps them treat patients but also benefits them personally, in the long run.

Cognitive Behavioral Therapy was originally designed specifically for treating patients with depression. However, its use has expanded over the years and Cognitive Behavioral Therapy helps people suffering from many different kinds of problems. It works like a psycho-social intervention that is focused on changing a person's negative thoughts, beliefs, and behaviors by improving their emotional processing ability and development of better coping strategies.

When people become more aware of their thinking patterns, it helps them to bring about profound changes in their lives. These changes may seem small at first, but their impact is significant. Most people have their share of anxiety, low moods, stress, etc. at some point in their lives. So, if you think about it, Cognitive Behavioral Therapy can help every one of us. The tools of Cognitive Behavioral Therapy help to deal with so many issues and also to prevent them from recurring in the future.

People will have different reasons for seeking out Cognitive Behavioral Therapy. A lot of them might have already tried other treatments but not found them to be effective enough. Some might have noticed that they are still avoiding situations that are uncomfortable when they should be facing them. Some people want to counter their habit of self-criticism with self-love. Some people may be completely unaware of their issues or are living in denial. However, a lot of people who want to start Cognitive Behavioral Therapy are those who are well aware of their issues and are looking for the tools or skills that will help them address these issues once and for all. They know that Cognitive Behavioral Therapy can be a type of therapy that can help them transform the insight they already have into real change. I personally recommend Cognitive Behavioral Therapy to as many people as possible, and all the time, because I know how it works and believe it can help so many more.

Some people don't seek out therapy or any professional help because they feel like their problems are just too big to be solved by a therapist. They think that a psychologist or therapist can only help someone with insomnia get a prescription for a few sleeping pills. They don't trust someone else to understand or solve their own seemingly larger problems. However, it is only self-destructive to keep these things locked away. Every person can benefit from Cognitive Behavioral Therapy, in one way or another. It may not solve your whole problem and make it go completely away, but it will help you to manage your struggles in a much better way.

If you want to get started with Cognitive Behavioral Therapy with some support, we suggest looking for a good therapist. Look around and ask people for recommendations. Find someone who will make you comfortable even as they challenge you to change for the better. A good therapist will listen to you and validate your perspective. They will challenge you gently when required but will also provide you a safe haven to speak openly without being judged. You will know a good therapist when you meet one.

If you look at the principles of Cognitive Behavioral Therapy, you will see that it borrows from the principles of Cognitive Psychology and Behavioral Psychology. However, Cognitive Behavioral Therapy is much more focused on problems and taking actions to resolve them.

It is a much newer concept compared to other older psychotherapy programs. It falls under the second wave of psychotherapy and its popularity has only been growing.

For instance, at first, therapists were focused on studying the behavior of a person to find the hidden meaning behind it and this helped them to diagnose the problem. However, in Cognitive Behavioral Therapy, the therapist will be much more focused on treating the issues that specifically arise due to the mental illness that the client is suffering from. Effective strategies are used to help patients achieve certain goals. These Cognitive Behavioral Therapy strategies are known to decrease symptoms of the disorder they face and improve their way of life. It involves learning coping mechanisms and some skills that will help them reduce the effect of these diagnosed diseases. Cognitive Behavioral Therapy theories suggest that most psychological disorders are linked to distortion in thought processes and maladaptive behavior. This is why the therapy is quite focused on changing the way the person thinks so that it does not result in any maladaptive behavior. So you can see that Cognitive Behavioral Therapy is less focused on diagnosing a particular disease and more on finding solutions to whatever is ailing the patient.

Another benefit of Cognitive Behavioral Therapy is that it is extremely effective even at times when psychoactive medication is not used. This kind of treatment can be used to help a person recover from some mild addictions, stress, anxiety, and personality disorders. Cognitive Behavioral Therapy will also help adults or children who may display aggressive tendencies and help them improve their behavior. Medication is used in combination with Cognitive Behavioral Therapy when the client is suffering from more severe forms of any of these conditions. For instance, a therapist will most likely prescribe psychoactive medication when a person suffers from major depression, bipolar disorder, or obsessive-compulsive disorder. In fact, all psychiatry residents have a compulsory training of Cognitive Behavioral Therapy and interpersonal psychotherapy during their course.

Like we mentioned already, Cognitive Behavioral Therapy is a combination of Behavioral therapy with Cognitive therapy. Now let's try to understand what each of these involve individually.

Cognitive Therapy

This therapy was first developed by an American psychiatrist named Aaron T. Beck. He said that there is a link between a person's thoughts and feelings and their behavior. This is why it would be ineffective to study any of these aspects individually and much better to do a combined study. According to him, this would be a more effective way of understanding the client and diagnosing their condition. Appropriate treatment can only be suggested when the right condition is diagnosed. This is how Cognitive Therapy was developed. It is focused on present thinking and behavior, along with communication. It is less focused on a person's past experiences and helps them instead learn how to overcome issues in the present. There are a wide range of issues that are treated with the help of Cognitive Therapy. These include anxiety, depression, eating disorders, panic, and substance abuse.

Behavioral Therapy

Behavioral Therapy involves studying behavioral patterns to understand a person's mental state. This is more of an umbrella term for different types of mental health therapies. It is focused on identifying and changing any unhealthy and potentially self-destructive behaviors in a person. The basic principle is that it believes that all behavior is learned and any unhealthy behavior can be unlearned and changed. In this therapy, an individual's behavior will be observed in response to different stimuli and different types of situations. The therapist will especially focus on the different situations that a person will usually go through in their day-to-day lives. This helps them to identify the cause of the issues and then they can help the client find a way to deal with them and solve the problems.

The combination of Behavioral Therapy and Cognitive Therapy came to be one of the best psychotherapeutic methods used in recent years. Instead of trying a single treatment, it allowed the therapist to combine two effective treatments to get better results. Cognitive Behavioral Therapy emphasizes how logic and reason could not be the only factors to treat mental disorders. There are other logic-defying factors that also have to be taken into consideration. When it comes to mental health, it is also not possible to solve issues singularly with medication. There are various factors that have to be considered, and different treatments need to be tried to reach the crux of the issue and solve it.

History of Cognitive Behavioral Therapy

The various aspects of Cognitive Behavioral Therapy originated from many different philosophical traditions of old. One main source of influence was Stoicism, and a lot of the principles of Cognitive Behavioral Therapy are borrowed from it. In Stoicism, it was taught that logic could be used to get rid of any false beliefs that led to destructive emotions in a person. You can see the similarity to identifying and treating cognitive distortions here. These philosophies from Stoicism were often referred to by Aaron T. Beck, who is known as the father of Cognitive Therapy. Some other significant people who endorsed Cognitive Behavioral Therapy were Albert Ellis and John Stuart Mill. One of the first few therapists to recommend Cognitive Therapy was Alfred Adler. His work later influenced Albert Ellis, who then developed Rational Emotive Behavior Therapy. This REBT treatment was the earliest cognition based psychotherapy. Beck was the one who said that Freud's theory did not apply in every single instance and that certain thoughts could be the cause of emotional distress in any person.

Cognitive Therapy was developed from this type of thinking, and this is where they referred to automatic thoughts. Studies on conditioning were conducted around the year 1920 by Rayner and Watson. These were an important part of behaviorism studies. It was around 1960 that Cognitive Therapy was founded but Behavioral Therapy dated as far back as the early 1900s. Older studies were used to develop Behavioral Therapy further by Joseph Wolfe.

A whole lot more of research was conducted in later years by the likes of Glenn Wilson and Arnold Lazarus. Watson, Pavlov, and Hull put forward a theory that inspired a lot more studies on Cognitive and Behavioral Therapy. It soon started being used in different countries around the world. The work of Joseph Wolfe was extremely significant in laying the foundation for fear reduction techniques that are still being used today. Rotter and Bandura were other contributors whose main work was on the Social Learning Theory. They showed how learning and behavior modification were impacted by cognition. The emphasis on behavioral factors contributed to the first wave of Cognitive Behavioral Therapy being used. REMT, as well as Cognitive Therapy, caused the second wave. The third wave was a result of blending technical applications with theory from Behavioral and Cognitive Therapy. This should give you a brief idea of the origins of Cognitive Behavioral Therapy.

CONCLUSION

In this book we have taught you what cognitive behavioral therapy is as well as how to find a good therapist that can meet your needs and covering what actually happens in a session so that you have as much information as possible before making the decision to begin this type of therapy. By having this information, you may feel more at ease with the idea of therapy itself and feel less anxiety. We have given you the tools to understand what it is you are getting into as well as how long this type of therapy usually lasts and the benefits that it can bring you. When you are able to understand what cognitive behavioral therapy is and how it can benefit you, you can start to heal yourself from the difficulties that plague you on a daily basis and the negative emotions that you might be drowning in so that you don't have to keep thinking these negative thoughts that plague you. It also helps you have ways to move past them and overcome them.

This will also help you understand that you don't have to keep fighting against them either and that there is a way to help these thoughts. With cognitive behavioral therapy, you can move past the difficulties that you are facing, and you can overcome them as well. We also understand that anxiety and depression are a very serious problem with many people and they're not getting the proper recognition in certain aspects. As such we've given you exercises to help you with them and explained how cognitive behavioral therapy can help with understanding these two issues and how to make them better. Depression and anxiety take a very long time to heal from because they are serious issues, but cognitive behavioral therapy is designed to help these two issues to make it more manageable and try to begin to help you conquer these issues. By beginning cognitive therapy, you will start to see that your depression and anxiety are becoming more manageable and you are becoming a more positive person which can help these issues.

Chapter 17 Facts Versus Opinions

This simple exercise revolves around a common misconception plenty of patients make. It can't be helped, though. Sometimes, panic and depression attacks make it almost impossible for us to get our thoughts straight.

When that happens, we are prone to making very big distortions about our beliefs. One thing becomes another and the next thing falls out of place entirely.

This same thing can be said about the difference between facts and opinions. When we are quick to register one as the other, we end up with unrealistic expectations about ourselves. If left uncorrected, they spiral downward and drag us into a slump.

The Remedy

Fortunately, the difference between fact and opinion is a very solid wall. This wall has very visible characteristics to the trained eye. The job of therapist is to help the patient see these characteristics in order to make the proper distinction.

For this technique to work, some journaling and writing is needed.

First, sit down with your therapist to write all your sentiments about certain events. Don't worry about categorizing them immediately, what's important at this point is to make a complete list of your cognitions.

These could be about a recent argument you had with a relative. It could also be another panic attack after your boss gave you additional work to finish. It could also be an interesting discussion you had with a friend. The good thing about this exercise is that it's applicable on a daily basis, making it an ideal therapy-cap after each session.

Procedure

Once you and your therapist have a list of your cognitions, go over each item to determine under which category they belong. Are they mere opinions? Or are they undeniable facts?

One good way to test each item is to give yourself reality checks. Ask yourself if each item can be refuted or not. See if you can present a counter-argument for each item. Here, you put on your thinking cap and question your own cognitions as if you were self-treating.

•   He hates you. Who told you that? Did he say that explicitly?

- You made a mistake. What criteria did you fail to meet?

- You're weak. What standards? Who gave you that assessment?

- You won't finish that report this week. According to who?

There is something amiss about you. What could it be? What makes it wrong? Does everybody think that way?

By questioning the items from your journal, you can determine which ones are opinions and which ones are facts.

Of course, facts are unchangeable, but you can change the way you view them. Opinions on the other hand, are more flexible and change depending on your current perspective.

The main purpose of this exercise is to show you the truth that thoughts are not facts. The way you think may be an honest representation of your internal conflict, but that is in no way empirical evidence of any of your anxiety disorder or depression-based claims.

The exercise is designed to teach you to reevaluate yourself from time to time, double-checking your cognitions to make sure that you don't run into any unhealthy distortions along the way.

For severe cases, this exercise becomes a life-saving technique that tells you to slow down and think things through with a rational mind. Coupled with the other techniques mentioned in this workbook, this exercise can also serve as a good test to see if you can distinguish fact from opinion in real time.

Chapter 18 Successive Approximation

In today's environment, we are no longer plagued by threats to our survival, unlike our ancestors. However, we face a new set of threats in this modern age that take on a different, but equally dangerous form.

Let's say that your in-laws will be spending a holiday with you and your partner for the weekend. With the knowledge that these people aren't particularly fond of you, this encounter can be a very stressful engagement.

Even at work, this can happen. What if your boss passes by your station and hands you a large pile of tasks that need to be finished by the end of the day, which is coupled by the myriad of things you are already doing. Imagine if your daily tasks were also in preparation for a big presentation that you have with that same supervisor the following day.

Do these scenarios seem too big to handle? Do they cause stress and anxiety disorder? Do the sizes of these tasks make them seem impossible to handle?

The same thing can be said about CBT. In fact, CBT was designed with approximation in mind.

Main Premise

Instead of looking at one, large, impossible task, breaking it down into simpler and doable tasks makes the large picture sound possible. This isn't just a work principle to make things easier. It's a premise that makes CBT possible.

At the start of therapy, you may be shocked by the amount of progress you're supposed to make within just a few weeks. All the homework and writing and self-inspection seems too much.

This may, in turn, cause additional stress and anxiety disorder on your end. How are you expected to get better so soon? How will you get over something that's been bothering you your whole life in just a matter of weeks?

You will do it in small increments. This is what the initial stage of CBT is for. It is meant for planning. It was designed as something both the therapist and patient do together so that the patient sees how something so massive can be very doable.

Application

With that principle in mind, it's easy to take approximation wherever you go. Take, for instance, the two problems mentioned at the beginning of this .

That holiday with the in-laws seems more doable when you break down the whole experience into smaller chunks. Preparing their itineraries and their meals ahead of time gives you less things to worry about when they arrive. Clearing out a room for them ahead of time also sounds like a good idea.

On top of that, planning activities for them that keep them away from you won't just do you good, but will also make their stay with you much more bearable. Suddenly, the trip doesn't look so intimidating anymore.

About that mountain of work that needs to be finished, it's easier when you take a step back and lay everything on the table.

What are all the tasks that you have to complete? When you've enumerated all these things, rank them in order of priority. Which ones should be completed first? Which ones are needed for completion immediately? Which tasks precede the others in importance?

With a priority list in place, you can effectively budget your time and effort to finish everything in a timely manner. And since you've already planned everything out, you won't have to worry about missing anything and making any mistakes along the way. This is the power of approximation.

Soon, almost every big task will look like a complicated set of interconnected tasks that can be broken down. When you've mastered this skill, very little can faze you and cause you stress and anxiety disorder.

Chapter 19 Anxiety and Depression Management

Expression often drains one's energy, drive, and hope, thus making it hard to do what one needs to feel better. Though overcoming depression is not easy or quick, it is not impossible. You cannot drive yourself to escape it, but you do have some control—though your depression may be stubbornly persistent and severe. The crucial factor is to start small then build up from there. It takes time so that one can start feeling better, but you can be there if you are willing to make for yourself positive choices every day.

Recovering from depression needs action but actioning when you are depressed is relatively hard. Just to think about the things one should do for them to feel better, such as hanging out with friends or going for a walk can be somehow exhausting. It is the vicious circle of depression recovery i.e. Those things that are most likely to help overcome depression are the most difficult ones to do. However, there is a difference between something that is difficult and something that is impossible. The most important thing when it comes to overcoming depression is to start by having some few small goals and gradually build up from there. Base and rely on whatsoever resources that you have. You might not have too much energy, but you possibly have enough to walk around your house or make a phone call to a loved one. Take things easy, living a day at a time as well as reward yourself for every accomplishment and achievement that you make. The steps might seem so small, but they will quickly tally up. For all the energy that you use in overcoming depression, you will get back much more in return.

Below are some six self-help tips that we believed are essential for you in this journey of coping up and overcoming depression without falling into the trap of a relapse.

Self-Help Tip Beat Negative Thinking

Normally, depression puts an undesirable and negative spin on everything one experiences, including the way one sees himself/herself, the circumstances he/she encounters, and his/her expectations for the future. You can never break out of the pessimistic mentality by "just thinking positive." Wishful thinking and happy thoughts will not cut it. The trick needed in this case is to substitute negative thoughts and opinions with more balanced feelings and thoughts. Try thinking outside yourself. Ask yourself whether you would say what you are thinking regarding yourself to others. If not, then stop being hard on yourself. Ponder on less punitive statements that give more realistic descriptions.

Stop perceiving yourself to be perfect and allow yourself to fall short of perfection. most depressed individuals are perfectionists, regarding and holding themselves to terribly high standards and they end up beating themselves up whenever they fail to meet their set standards. Combat this origin of self-imposed anxiety by trying to challenge your negative thoughts. Socialize with positive-minded people. Take note of how positive-minded people deal with their challenges, even if they are minor ones, like not finding a parking space. Then think of how you would have reacted if you were in the same situation. Even if you will pretend, try adopting their optimism as well as persistence when facing difficulty.

You may as well have a "negative thought log." Each time you experience some negative thought, write it down in a notebook and what stimulated /triggered it. Create time to review your log when in good moods. Then consider if the negative thoughts or negativity was truly necessary. Ask yourself if there is any other way to perceive the situation. Always remember to substitute negative thoughts and opinions with more balanced feelings and thoughts. In this manner, you will find it easy overcoming depression as well as coping up.

Self-Help Tip Get Support

Getting proper support that you need plays a huge role in "lifting the fog" of anxiety and depression and taking it away from you. It can be very difficult to maintain perceptions and sustain the required energy to beat depression on your own, but again the depression's nature makes it somehow difficult to stretch out for help from others. Nevertheless, loneliness and isolation worsen depression, hence maintaining those close relationships as well as social activities are very important. The thought of even stretching out to very close family members can seem to be devastating. One may feel guilty, ashamed, or even too exhausted to talk. When having such thoughts always keep in mind that that is the depression talking to you. Reaching out to others is not an indication to show one's weakness and it will not mean that you are a burden to others. Remember that your loved ones care so much about you and would wish to help. Keep in mind that it is never late for one to build new healthy friendships and improve their support network.

Turn to your family members and trusted friends. Share with them what you are going through face to face talk if possible. The individuals you talk to do not have to sort you out immediately; they only need to be great listeners. Ask for support and help that you need. You might have withdrawn from your most cherished relationships, but be rest assured they may get you through the tough times. Try keeping up with social events even if you do not feel like it. Mostly when one is depressed, it always feels more comfortable retreating into their shell, but being around may make them feel less depressed. you may register and join a depression support group. Being with other people trying to battle depression can help in reducing one's sense of isolation. In such a group there is room for sharing personal experiences hence there is a higher likelihood of encouraging each other and giving and receiving advice on how to cope.

Self-Help Tip Take Care of Yourself To overcome depression, we ought to take good care of ourselves. This entails adopting healthy habits, having a healthy lifestyle, scheduling fun events into our day, learning to overcome stress, and setting boundaries on what one can do. Aim for at least 8hours of sleep every day. Depression stereotypically involves sleeping disorders. Whether one sleeps too much or too little, his or her mood suffers. Formulate a better sleeping schedule by practicing healthy sleep habits.

Ensure that every day you do expose yourself to some little sunlight. Not having enough sunlight or lack of it can make worsen one's depression. Get enough of it as much as possible. Take a random short walk outdoors, enjoy an outdoor meal, relax on a park bench, sit out in the garden, or even take your coffee outside. Aiming for at least fifteen minutes of sunlight in a day boosts one's mood. If you are living somewhere with very little winter sunshine, you can use a light therapy box. Always try to keep stress in check. Stress does not only worsen and prolong depression, but it triggers it. Always know and understand all the things that stress you out in your life. This might include unsupportive relationships, health problems, or work overload. Once you have identified your stressors, create a plan to minimize their impact or avoid them.

Continually practice the so far learned relaxation techniques. Doing the relaxation practice daily can help in relieving symptoms of depression, reducing stress, and boosting feelings of joy as well as our well-being. Try out yoga, progressive muscle relaxation, deep breathing, or meditation.

Care for a pet. Although nothing can in any way replace the human connection, our pets can bring companionship and joy into our lives and help us feel less isolated. Hence, taking care of a pet can as well get you back to yourself and give you some sense and feeling of being needed—a powerful antidote to depression.

Do the things you (used to) enjoy. While you cannot force yourself onto having fun or experiencing pleasure, you can always choose to do the things that you used to enjoy. Try out a sport or former hobby you used to love most. Paint the town red with friends. Creatively express yourself through art, music, or writing. Take a tour to a museum, the ballpark, or the mountains. Push yourself into doing things, even if you do not feel like it. You will be astonished at how you will feel, much better, once you are out in the world. Though your depression might not lift instantly, you will slowly feel more energetic and cheerful as you create time for the fun activities.

Self-Help Tip Get Regular Exercises

When one is depressed, exercising might be the last thing that he/she would feel like doing. Exercising is a useful and powerful tool for overcoming depression. Research indicates that regular exercises can be as efficient as antidepressant medication at lowering feelings of fatigue and increasing one's energy levels.

Scientists have not found out exactly the reason behind exercise being such a powerful antidepressant, nevertheless evidence shows that physical activity stimulates the growth of new cells in the brain, relieves muscle tension, increases mood-enhancing endorphins and neurotransmitters, and reduces stress. All these are things that have a positive impact on depression. Aim at doing exercise for at least 30 minutes per day to get the most benefits. Though you can start small by doing activities as short as 10minutes as it will have a positive impact on your mood. Below are a few easy steps to get you moving:

•	Climb up through the stairs rather than using an elevator

•	Walk around the house while making a phone call

•	Pair up/get an exercise partner

• In the parking lot, park your car at the farthest spot.

Keep in mind to always incorporate walks and other forms of exercise and activities into your daily program/routine. The most important clue at this point is that you pick an activity or event that you enjoy most so that you are likelier to keep up with it.

Self-Help Tip Eat a Healthy Diet

What one eats directly impacts the way he or she feels. Aim at taking a balanced diet that is made up of low-fat proteins, fruits, vegetables, and complex carbohydrates. Lessen your consumption of foods that may negatively affect your mood or brain, such as alcohol, caffeine, saturated fats, and foods that have high chemical preservatives level or hormones.

Do not skip your meals. Aim at eating something at least after every 3 to 4 hours as going for a long period between your meals might make you feel tired and irritable.

Minimize refined carbs and sugar. You may desire or have a craving for baked goods, sugary snacks, or comfort foods like French fries or pasta, but these foods quickly bring about lowering energy levels and crash in one's mood.

Concentrate on complex carbohydrates. Increase your intake on foods such as whole-wheat pasta, baked potatoes, whole-grain breads, and oatmeal as they can enhance serotonin levels without causing a crash. Increase your vitamins intake, eat more leafy greens, citrus fruit, eggs, chicken, and beans. Try taking super-foods that are rich in nutrients for boosting mood, like spinach, brown rice, and bananas.

Omega-3 fatty acids can as well play a vital role in steadying and stabilizing one's mood. Some of the best sources are fatty fish, for instance, salmon, mackerel, anchovies, sardines, and herring. When preparing fish, you would rather bake or grill rather than fry them.

Self-Help Tip Know When to Get Further Help

If your depression gets worse and worse, do not hesitate to look out for assistance from professionals. Needing additional help does not mean that you are weak. At times the negative thoughts in depression might make you feel like you are a lost cause, nevertheless, the good news is that depression is treatable, and you will feel better!

Chapter 20 Let Go of Self-Centered Narratives

Now that you have a rough collection of the stories or personal scripts that you play in your mind constantly, the next step is to let go of some of them.

It should be obvious that not all the narratives that you play consistently in your head do you good. In fact, if you're reading this book, there's a decent chance that a lot of them are harming you or frustrated. Maybe they make you feel small, powerless, or 'stuck.' Perhaps you feel some of your narratives are holding you back from your fullest potential. Whatever the case may be, these personal stories that you use to filter reality are somehow preventing you from living a life of consistent victory.

In this, we're going to let go of the low-hanging fruit as far as your negative or not so optimal narratives are concerned. We're going to let go of the most obviously counterproductive first.

As I mentioned in there is one type of personal narrative that is absolutely toxic-self-absorption. According to this personal script, the whole world-even the universe-revolves around you, your need for comfort, your desire for convenience, your sense of fairness, and everything else you feel you deserve. Obviously, the world doesn't revolve around you. Accordingly, you have to let go.

Again, spoiler alert: the world is not about you. The world has its own agenda. The world spins on its own axis regardless of your feelings. No matter how hard you wish or try, the world is not going away any time soon. You, on the other hand, have a definite expiration date.

Most human beings do not live beyond the age of 130. That's just the mortal limit that we all have to face sooner rather than later. The world, on the other hand, will probably continue unless we ourselves choose to blow it up.

Understand how this all works. Understand your place in the cosmic order of things. Understand your magnitude and how small you are in light of everything else that is happening.

If you're having a tough time wrapping your mind around this, I want you to play this little mental exercise. I want you to close your eyes and imagine looking at yourself in the room where you're reading this book. See the image> You see somebody 20 feet away from reading this book. Got it? Now zoom out one mile, so that you see yourself in a neighborhood or a city, surrounded by buildings, reading that book. There are a lot of people around you, but you can still see yourself in that building.

Now zoom out a hundred miles. Looking down from the sky, you can see the state or region you're in surrounded by other nearby regions. Zoom out 300 miles and you see the country that you're in, and neighboring countries. Zoom out some more and you see the continent your country is in. Zoom out a hundred thousand miles, and you see the earth. All of it. What a beautiful blue orb floating in the vast blackness that is space. Don't get too attached though... Proceed to zoom out one million miles, and you see the earth revolving around the Sun. Zoom out ten million miles and you see the sun mostly. You barely see the earth.

Do you see my point? If you are to zoom out enough, you see our solar system, and then you see the galaxies, and so forth. I don't mean to make you feel worthless by pointing out how small we all really are. My point is that you need to have the proper perspective. Being tiny and part of a larger cosmic play over which you really have no power over is perfectly okay. It really is. Why?

That smallness in the big scheme of things is our shared reality.

You need to zero in on the smallness of your being. You're only here for, in light of Earth's geographic age and history, a blink of an eye. If you look at how long the universe has been around, and consider how long you've been alive, you don't even register. That's how small you are. That's the point in history you occupy.

All this political drama of people getting elected, assassinated, revolutions, wars of religion – you name it-and all the emotional intensity and drama it all brings, ultimately amounts to nothing. We're just a momentary detail in space and time as far as Earth is concerned. And I haven't even started talking about the age of the universe! The verdict? We're only a tiny blip.

Again, I don't mean to destroy your sense of importance, I just need you to develop a humbler, less self-centered perspective because a little humility goes a long way. You don't have to be Atlas. You don't have to be a demi-god holding up the world on your shoulders. You can shrug the world off your shoulders. It's perfectly okay, because that's not your job.

It's not your job to be the center of the universe. It's not your job to be the conscious filter of everything that exists today. That should not be your perspective. Instead, you need to welcome the narrative that you are just a passing entity in this grand play that has gone on for billions of years before you were even born and will go on for a very long time to come. And it's all perfectly okay.

The world is not about you. The world has its own history and trajectory. It is perfectly okay to just let go. You need to let go of that narrative where you are constantly the center of everything. Everything happening in your life doesn't have to be a judgment of you. Everything doesn't have to involve your feelings. Step away from that. Humility-that sense of smallness-is the key that will turn the lock on this toxic mental prison door.

Conclusion

I want to pat you on the back for finishing this book and completing the above homework assignments! The fact that you are motivated to changing your life and mindset for the better says so much about your character! This will make a world of difference in the months to come as you fight against negativity and embrace positivity and change.

Even changing for the better is difficult to manage. That said, I remind you to be gentle with yourself as you venture into a more positive outlook and as you completely change your lease on life.

Now what? The next step is to take the abundance of knowledge you have acquired from reading this book and put it into practice in your everyday life. The best way to make any change, big or small, is to start making baby-like strides. This will help you to succeed faster as you eliminate darkness and embrace a much lighter mindset.

• Instead of becoming automatically overwhelmed when assigned big projects at work or home, look at them differently. Break them down into bite-sized chunks and complete each task, one at a time. You will fulfill that project with positivity still intact.

•   Tough times in your relationship? Don't talk bad about your significant other, family member, or friend to others. This will just wreak more havoc. Instead, nip the issues you have with them in the bud. Talk to them personally and erase any bad feelings/actions. It will feel as if a boulder is lifted from you.

•   Have you fallen into rough financial waters? What are the small steps you can take to get you back afloat?

As you have learned, cognitive behavioral therapy is made up of small but important pieces that help you to change your entire outlook of how you perceive life each day. When done correctly, you will notice that life ultimately gets better and is really is not how you have cracked it up to be.

A long conclusion, but I wanted to leave you with a few thoughts before you put this knowledge away and never use it! It is important to take care of yourself, both physically and mentally, for they both go hand-in-hand to determine the kind of life you lead.

I hope this book was not only informative but a good time to read, and that it was able to provide you with all of the tools you need to achieve your goals to live a happier, more fulfilled life!